Britain and Europe: The Untold History

– RICHARD ELLIS –

An environmentally friendly book printed and bound in England by
www.printondemand-worldwide.com

http://www.fast-print.net/bookshop

BRITAIN AND EUROPE: THE UNTOLD HISTORY

A catalogue record for this book is available from the British Library

ISBN 978-178456-331-8

Also available as e-book:
ePub ISBN: 9781784569464
Mobi ISBN: 9781784569471

First published 2016 by
FASTPRINT PUBLISHING
Peterborough, England.

Britain and Europe: *The Untold History*

A millennium of conquest, revolution and leadership – and what it can teach us

By Richard Ellis

INTRODUCTION

"The end of a thousand years of history…"

So said Labour Leader Hugh Gaitskell of the suggestion that Britain should join the European Economic Community. Many Britons share that view today. Plenty of conquerors have tried, runs the logic, and we have sent them all packing. Not since 1066 have we lain beneath the conqueror's boot. This idea lies deep in the British psyche and helps explain our dislike of the European project. What, after all, was the point of seeing off Philip II's Spanish Armada, Napoleon's Grande Armée and Hitler's Luftwaffe only to end up under the sway of Brussels' bureaucrats? When we say a thousand years of history we mean a millennium of independence. Alas, wonderful though it sounds, this rather over-eggs the pudding.

We may have banished them from our collective memory but there have been a number of occasions on which English and, later, British sovereignty has been lost to European powers.

King John sold England's crown to the Pope and turned us into a subjugated papal province. Mary I imposed a Spanish king upon us and watched as England was dragged into Spanish wars. Charles II concluded a secret treaty with the King of France and, in doing so, gave Paris the final say over England's religious and foreign policies.

However, if these were occasions on which we lost political sovereignty, they were also occasions on which we fought to get it back.

The Magna Carta barons waged revolutionary war against John and the Pope. Great statesmen tried to restrict the political power of Queen Mary's husband. An ambitious House of Commons rumbled Charles' secret treaty and responded by seizing significant (albeit temporary) control over both foreign and domestic policy.

These forgotten episodes have much to teach us about the nature, and precious fragility, of political sovereignty.

In addition to the history that we forget is the history that we misremember. The Glorious Revolution and the Hanoverian Succession fall into this category. At school we are taught that the former was all about freeing ourselves from the Catholic despotism of James II and that the latter introduced a foreign king whose disinterest allowed ministerial and parliamentary power to grow. Both events are seen as triumphs for our national interest. This view is accurate up to a point but it is far from the whole truth.

William III and George I were both prepared to spend English blood and treasure on furthering the ambitions of their home countries and there were certainly instances when England's interests were subordinated to those of Holland and Hanover. We will have to ask, as did the politicians of the time, whether these compromises were worthwhile or whether they represented a bad bargain.

As we review these episodes we will see that questions of sovereignty and questions of national interest are closely entwined and need careful, joint consideration.

The mythical "thousand years", however, are not just about sovereignty and national interest – they are also about distance. We like to think that, when we have not been defending ourselves from European invaders, we have been standing gloriously aloof from European politics. This was simply not the case.

Take the Napoleonic Wars. While we rightly remember how Britain thrashed France, we tend to be less mindful of the fact that she did so at the head of a Europe-wide coalition. Pitt the Younger, Lord Nelson and the Duke of Wellington were obviously British heroes but they were also European leaders. They worked with European allies and commanded European armies. Other British statesmen, too, have played active, positive and decisive roles in European history.

Lord Palmerston is one such. Palmerston may have been a fan of gunboat diplomacy but he also worked tirelessly and successfully to champion Britain's liberal allies against the autocracies of Austria, Prussia and Russia. Dictatorships would have loomed even larger in nineteenth-century Europe had it not been for Palmerston. Lord Salisbury and Benjamin Disraeli may be considered here too. These men saved Europe from all-out war by providing a workable compromise to the Eastern Question and by forcing Europe to accept this compromise at the Congress of Berlin.

Britain has done more good for Europe than we remember and we have more to offer the European Union than some people think. After all, the reforms that Britain wishes to see (restoring powers to national parliaments, cutting regulation and pursuing free trade deals around the world) would not just benefit Britain, they would benefit all EU member states.

As we approach the referendum on 23rd June we will once again have to weigh up considerations of sovereignty against those of our national interest more broadly. We may conclude that the EU takes too much of the former while adding too little to the latter. We may decide that the EU writes too many of our laws without making us sufficiently better off. David Cameron's renegotiation improved the situation but has not totally redressed the balance. A Leave vote currently[1] looks highly sensible. Most British people, however, would only cast such a vote with a good deal of wariness. We know that leaving the EU would bring difficulties and dangers of its own. Many of us are leaning towards "Leave" but could be persuaded to "Remain". The question is what the EU will do to win us over.

---

[1] Writing at the end of February 2016

It is worth remembering the Scottish independence referendum of 2014. The referendum campaign itself was crucial and negotiations effectively went right to the wire. It was, after all, only two days before the vote when the leaders of the three main Westminster parties made their "Vow" offering more power to Scotland in the event that the Scots voted to stay in the United Kingdom. Something similar could well happen in the EU referendum.

As the debate develops and minds begin to concentrate, it is likely that some in Brussels will see the need to offer better terms to Britain. In the concluding chapter of this book we will explore this possibility in greater detail and consider how to make the most of it. Again, we will be able to find much help from our history.

It may well be that the run-up to the referendum will provide opportunities for British-inspired reforms. If the EU refuses to change then Britain may well leave. If the EU takes its lead from Britain then we might remain and the EU as a whole will be better off. As so often before, Britain has the right ideas and is ready to lead. The question is whether Europe is ready to follow.

Before we start planning for the future, however, we need to understand the lessons of the past...

PART I – SOVEREIGNTY

King John and the Golden Bull

Like me, you probably first met King John when he, and the wicked Sheriff of Nottingham, were being outsmarted by Robin Hood, Friar Tuck and the rest of Sherwood Forest's Merry Men. In the Robin Hood stories John is depicted as cowardly, selfish and deceitful. Sometimes folk tales embellish and distort; they do not do so here. In this case the fictional apple has not fallen far from the factual tree. Most of us think of John as a villain of almost pantomime proportions. We are right to do so.

This was a man who waged war against his father and who tried to usurp the crown from his crusading brother. He very likely had his nephew murdered and he was not above punishing the wives and the children of those who offended him. It is nothing short of proper to label John a villain.

Nor was villainy John's only failing. He was a thoroughly incompetent monarch. His handling of foreign policy was particularly inept. By a series of blunders, John managed to get himself into a position where he was fighting both the King of France and the Pope. As such he faced the very real prospect of losing his throne and his life. Unable to face both of his foes, he chose to submit to one. As if villainy and incompetence were not enough, the King would now turn traitor. Backed into a corner, John would betray his people by transferring England's sovereignty to Rome. John yielded the kingship of England to the Pope and received the crown back as the Pope's feudal tenant. The terms of this surrender would have profound and far-reaching consequences – not least for Magna Carta.

In this chapter, as we see John turn England into an outpost of the Papacy, we will see how short-sighted it is to think that England has been free for a thousand years. We will see how England's freedom was lost and we will see how it was regained. First, however, we need to understand something of John's situation when he came to the throne in 1199.

John's paternal grandfather was Geoffrey, Count of Anjou. By the usual medieval techniques of fighting well and marrying even better, Geoffrey and his son, Henry II of England, had amassed a formidable collection of lands. John was Henry's son and, when he became King of England, he also inherited a clutch of French titles and possessions. He became, inter alia, Duke of Normandy, Count of Anjou and lord of Auvergne, Brittany, Gascony, Guienne, Limousin and Saintogne. History has described this as the Angevin Empire. The word Angevin derives from the family's early possessions in Anjou but it is on the word Empire that we should focus, for it is deeply misleading. John was no Emperor.

True, John was at the top of the tree in England, but he had a much lower place in the French pecking order. France, like the other nations of medieval Europe, was a feudal kingdom. This conditioned John's relations with the French King. In a feudal monarchy, the king is the biggest of the big cheeses and controls all the land. He then parcels out portions of this land to senior nobles and churchmen. In return, these "tenants-in-chief" agree to provide soldiers and money when required. When things went to plan, kings did rather well out of this arrangement; but things did not always go to plan. Tenants-in-chief were powerful figures and, if they decided to be uppity, feudal kings could find themselves in tricky spots. Uppitiness has never been a stranger to the French national character and French kings often found themselves in tricky spots with their tenants-in-chief. Geoffrey of Anjou and Henry II of England had been among the worst offenders. The kings of France had grown weary of having half their kingdom effectively ruled by kings of England who refused to accept that, as Dukes of Normandy, they were feudal tenants. Philip II of France wanted to bring the Angevins to heel – and he was on the lookout for any excuse for war.

The situation was unstable and John's hold on power was precarious. He would have to tread very carefully if he was to avoid provoking war with France. Unfortunately, John was temperamentally incapable of treading carefully. John was soon ready for marriage and his choice of bride was to prove explosive. John had fallen for Isabella of Angoulême.

Isabella was an attractive prospect. In addition to being a beautiful young lady of noble birth, she was also a considerable heiress. Even better, from John's point of view, was the fact that she held a set of estates conveniently located between his own possessions in Poitou and Gascony. One can readily understand why the King had designs on Isabella. The course of true love, however, never does run smooth – especially when political considerations are thrown into the mix. The problem in this case was that Isabella was already engaged to Hugh de Lusignan. Hugh was the son of the Count of Le Marche, a powerful French nobleman. Had John stopped to think, he would have realised that seeking Isabella's hand would be a perilous enterprise and that the potential dangers outweighed the likely gains. John, however, was always more of an "act now, think later" kind of monarch. Throwing caution to the wind, he wed Isabella and dared the de Lusignans to challenge him. He would not have to wait long.

As soon as the marriage was announced, Hugh and his father went tattling to their feudal lord, Philip of France. They were canny in the wording of their complaint. They did not say that they had been wronged by the King of England. Rather, they claimed that Hugh had been mistreated by the Count of Poitou (another of John's titles). The King of England would have been outside of Philip's jurisdiction. The Count of Poitou was very much within that jurisdiction. The French King lost no time in summoning John to attend a feudal court in France. Philip must have been delighted. The de Lusignans had furnished him just the basis he needed to take action against John. While notionally seeking justice for one of his subjects, Philip could judge and punish John as he wished.

Nor was that thought lost on John. When he received Philip's summons, John could hardly have envisaged that he would receive a fair trial. Philip would exact a terrible price in land or treasure (or, more likely, both) and make John look a fool to boot. John took the only sensible course open to him. He refused to attend. Philip pressed the point. Legally Philip must have been right but John could not budge. In not attending his lord when commanded, the Count of Poitou had breached a basic feudal duty. Philip had his excuse for war.

The campaign was one of considerable twists and turns. John got off to a bad start but Philip overreached himself and sought to capture Eleanor of Acquitaine, John's mother, at Mirabeau Castle. Fired by filial sentiment, John put in a barnstorming performance at the Battle of Mirabeau, managing both to defeat Philip's forces and to capture most of the opposing generals. This was to be the high watermark of John's campaigns in France.

Not only did things deteriorate from here, but they did so to a terrible extent and with a dizzying speed.

A big part of the problem was that John was a total imbecile. He should have been flat-out charming his current allies and trying to add to his collection of supporters. Instead he kept putting people's backs up. Not only that but, having captured a group of enemy noblemen, he went on to treat them so badly that nearly two dozen of them died. Noble families often intermarried, so John had allowed relatives of his actual and potential allies to die of neglect. This was no way to win friends and influence people. A number of vital allies deserted him when they learnt the news. As ally followed ally down the rat run to Philip, those who remained felt decreasingly confident that they were backing a winner and many more promptly cleared off. However, if his shabby and cruel behaviour had cost John support, his reputation was about to be further tarnished by accusations of sheer barbarism.

One of the generals whom John had captured was a young prince called Arthur. Arthur was the son of John's older brother Geoffrey. As such, Arthur had a strong claim to John's crown and estates. If John were to lose the war, Philip would very likely install Arthur in his place. What would John do now that he had Arthur in his hands?

While no one can be absolutely sure of Arthur's fate, the balance of opinion, both at the time and subsequently, was that John had Arthur killed.

Now these were not gentle times. Wars were frequent and bloody. Kings (and pretenders) often led their troops from the front and could expect to be slain in battle. However, there was a world of difference between dealing the death blow to a fellow warrior on the field of honour and bumping off a defenceless captive in his prison cell. When that prisoner was of royal blood and the nephew of the killer you have a flagrant and scandalous breach of the chivalric code. You also have a PR nightmare. John's stock was already low, but the suspicion that he callously murdered a relative (believed by some to be the rightful King of England) sent it nose-diving. Yet more allies deserted him and, despite some gutsy soldiering and a savage campaign in Brittany, John's cause in France was done for. He retreated to England. He had lost Poitou and Normandy. He had also lost the ancestral county that had given the Angevin Empire its name and which had remained its heartland: Anjou was gone. He was left with nothing but Acquitaine. And when his mother died his hold there began to look shaky too.

The war had already been of protracted duration and both sides were growing tired of the conflict. John and Philip agreed an uneasy truce. This should have brought a welcome period of relief. John should have seized it with both hands. He should have taken the opportunity to pause and regroup. His focus should have been on maintaining a maximum level of calm to allow his armies recover their strength. John, ever his own worst enemy, chose this moment to blunder into a conflict with the Pope.

The nub of the dispute was the appointment of the Archbishop of Canterbury. John's favoured candidate had been John de Gray, Bishop of Norwich. This had been communicated to Pope Innocent III and John had expected the appointment to be rubber-stamped. Innocent had other ideas. The Pope appointed Stephen Langton. John was furious.

The last thing John needed was to have another fight in his hands but he simply could not help himself. As if the King of France were not enough, he now decided to take on the Roman Catholic Church. John's opening salvo was to forbid Langton to enter England. He followed this up by confiscating various archiepiscopal lands. Innocent could not let this pass and was quick to deploy the power of the Holy See. The Pope put England under an Interdict.

The Interdict prevented priests from conducting the vast majority of Church services. The clergy were allowed to baptise the young, to give the last rites to the dying and hear confessions from the rest but that was it. The service of Holy Communion could not be celebrated. The people of England could probably have coped without matins, but the fact that they were unable to marry and that their dead were denied Christian burial was a much greater loss. When Innocent went onto excommunicate John, England looked a Godless realm indeed.

This was not just a problem for the souls of John's subjects, it was a threat to the security of his rule. If England was deemed to have severed itself from Christendom then winning it back would be a holy cause. John soon learnt that Philip of France was preparing to don the crusader's tunic and invade England to deliver her people from the tyrannous rule of their sacrilegious King. John knew that Philip would find money and allies much more easily if his venture had been blessed by Rome. When Philip next attacked it could well be with overwhelming force.

John was in a bind. In Philip and Innocent he had been facing two separate foes and he had just about been holding the line against both. Fighting them together could well prove ruinous. To a more principled man, the situation would have been fatal. John, however, was possessed of guile and shamelessness on a breathtaking scale. And he could see a way out. If he could not fight both then he would only fight one. In order only to fight one he would have to surrender to the other. He could not surrender to Philip without making significant territorial sacrifices. He could, however, surrender to the Pope. It would mean an epic climb-down but it could be pulled off without any of the tangible losses of his only other option. John would submit to Rome. This was a U-turn of staggering proportions.

We are talking, after all, about a king who reigned over a land where the church bells were silent. He had seized an array of Church properties and he had been excommunicated. Now he proposed to become the Pope's best friend. He would proclaim his loyalty to the Vicar of Christ. But he would not do so simply on a spiritual level. This was not a point of abstract theology. John would pledge himself to be the Pope's temporal servant. He would offer the throne of England to Innocent III and accept it back as Innocent's feudal vassal. In addition to accepting Innocent as his master, John agreed to return the lands and properties that he had confiscated and to pay the Papacy 1000 marks a year by way of tribute. All this was set out in a papal document called the Golden Bull. King John would agree to its terms in a lavish ceremony at the Temple Church at Dover.

There was panache aplenty and a host of leading figures. Great noblemen rubbed shoulders with senior prelates; aspirational clerks peeped over the shoulders of established courtiers. All wanted a good view of this once-in-a-lifetime event; a king was about to surrender his kingdom.

At one end of the chamber sat Pandulph, the Papal Legate. A distinguished gentleman clad head-to-foot in purple. In those more pious days, the Pope's claim to be the successor of St Peter and representative of Christ on Earth inspired greater awe than it does today. Admittedly they did not have the Pope himself, but to be in the same room as the representative of Christ's representative was no mean thing.

And here was the King. John advanced towards the Legate and knelt before him. This was a piece of profound political theatre. John was here to offer up his kingdom to the Pope. Pandulph, on His Holiness' behalf, accepted the English crown. For a moment, power was in transit and there was no king in England. Pandulph, however, was prepared to honour the bargain that had been struck and conveyed the royal authority back to John. John, grateful, rose and the ceremony was brought to an end. Whatever semi-mystical transfers of power had occurred, John left as he had arrived, King of England. But this was not, quite, the *status quo ante.* John was King again but he now undoubtedly had a master. As Count of Poitou, John had been Philip's vassal, but as King of England he tried to maintain that he was subordinate to nobody. This had completely changed. Now he was King of England precisely *because* he had accepted that he was subordinate to the Pope. It was a deeply shameful act.

John may have seen the Golden Bull as a tactical retreat but it had a deeper significance for his realm. England's ultimate sovereign now lived in Rome; she had been conquered by the Holy See. Of course the Pope had no military forces in England and could not dictate policy on a day-to-day basis, but the greatest questions of English politics could no longer be settled in England. We had become a papal territory and the Pope now had the last word. As in 1066, England had lost her independence.

John, however, was tickled pink. Any unity of purpose between Philip and the Pope had been pre-empted and, indeed, the Pope swung his support behind his new vassal. For a brief moment, things seemed to be looking up for John. Indeed, so pleased was John with how things were going that he launched an ill-starred bid to recapture Normandy. It was a foolish effort.

Even before he left England for France he must have seen that victory was unlikely. For a start his army was smaller than any he had led since coming to the throne. He had ordered his barons to muster, but many of his barons had stayed at home. They were a canny bunch. The barons took one look at John's abysmal battlefield record and realised that they were unlikely to find either glory or honour under his banner. Lacking this crucial support, John made a poor showing in Normandy and was soon sent packing. This defeat was too much for the barons. Those who had gone with him felt badly let down and those who had stayed in England were embarrassed at being led by a king who was on such familiar terms with military disaster.

John might have survived these foreign debacles if he had been a better ruler at home but his domestic policy had already pushed the barons to the brink. He had taxed them heavily and made a habit of exacting hefty fines for minor misdemeanours. His approach to justice had been capricious and those who had offended him had paid bitterly. John's barons were already ill-disposed towards him. Defeat in Normandy pushed them over the edge.

Renouncing their feudal duties to John, a collection of barons formed themselves into the rather grandly titled "Army of God and Holy Church". The Angevins, as tenants-in-chief across the Channel, had caused a great deal of trouble for their feudal overlord, the French King. Now the head of the House of Anjou was to get a taste of his own medicine. The rebellious barons had money and they had troops and they soon had John on the run. They took control of cities across the land and even seized London. With large portions of his country and even his own capital in rebel hands, John knew that he had to reach a compromise. He sued for peace. In exchange he was presented with the Articles of the Barons, known to history as Magna Carta.

The words "Magna Carta" echo down the centuries. This famous document stands as a triumph of the rule of law over royal absolutism and as a powerful statement of some essential freedoms. That said, we must be careful not to get carried away. Magna Carta was not an embryonic Charter of Human Rights and the barons who presented it to John were not the medieval equivalents of Shami Chakribarti.

Moreover, sad though it is to say, you will not find your heart leaping if you read Magna Carta today. It is as bereft of "the rights of man" as it is a stranger to "self-evident truths". In lots of ways it was a very parochial document. Many of the clauses are merely vehicles by which the barons sought redress for specific grievances. Even those aspects that do hint at broader applications (such as the guarantee that the King will not sell, delay or deny justice to any man) end up by disappointing. Quite apart from leaving women out altogether, this guarantee only operated in favour of freemen (not the villeins and serfs who made up so large a proportion of the population).

Nor should we make the mistake of thinking that the concept of limited monarchy that is set out in Magna Carta was an altogether novel one. The Anglo-Saxons (cousins, remember, of those German tribes who brought the western Roman Empire to its knees) had a sophisticated concept of liberty and this had not been wholly scotched by the Norman Conquest. Indeed, Magna Carta acknowledges the extent to which it is not a new departure. Article 1 simply *confirms* the rights and freedoms of the English Church. It does not claim that these rights and freedoms are being created in Magna Carta. This point is even more explicitly made in Article 13, which accepts the City of London's "ancient liberties". Whence these ancient liberties came is unstated but they clearly predate Magna Carta. It is no more true to say that English freedom began in 1215 than it is to agree with Philip Larkin and say that sexual intercourse began in 1963. In confirming that some freedoms were so hallowed by time and custom that not even the King could presume to be above them, Magna Carta was simply stating an existing principle. There were, however, some important innovations.

Article 14, for instance, prefigures a parliament to allow the King to take the common counsel of the realm. More important even than that was Article 61. Article 61 did represent a novel and powerful blow against royal authority. Under the terms of Article 61, the barons were to appoint a council of twenty-five of their number to superintend the performance of Magna Carta. The article even provided a procedure for a freeman to appeal to this council over the head of the King. It says that if the King or any of his ministers or officers breach any of the clauses in Magna Carta, then the wronged individual need simply bring this fact to the attention of four of the twenty-five barons so that those barons can inform the King and ask him to remedy the situation. That being done, the King has forty days (starting on the day on which he is notified of the breach) within which to correct matters. If he has failed to remedy the breach then the four barons should report back to the twenty-five. The council will then have power to act to enforce a remedy.

Magna Carta sets out the remarkable powers of the twenty-five in that circumstance. They shall be entitled to "distrain and distress [the king] in all possible ways, namely, by seizing [his] castles, lands, possessions, and in any other way they can, until redress has been obtained as they deem fit, saving harmless [his] own person, and the persons of [his] queen and children". That array of options should enable the twenty-five to provide redress to the wronged individual and Magna Carta states that when this has happened, the barons "shall resume their old relations towards [the king]". This was more than a limited monarchy. Article 61 set up a standing council to judge the behaviour of the King and to have almost unfettered power over his lands and possessions.

This was what Magna Carta added to the treasure-house of English liberties. It was not chiefly the liberties themselves. As we have seen, these were largely in existence already. Magna Carta's significance is in establishing whose responsibility it is to protect and enforce those liberties. Previously it could have been argued that it was the king's duty to observe and protect his subjects' freedoms. Magna Carta recognised that this was a romantic but flawed vision. After all, the king was himself one of the greatest threats to his subjects' liberty and it is plainly crackers to put the fox in charge of the henhouse. The Articles of the Barons represented the emergence of a political class beneath the King but with responsibilities that extended beyond those of the monarch. It would be this class that would take upon itself the responsibility for the defence of English freedom. Much of English history would amount to jockeying for position between this class and the sovereign. Alas, Magna Carta represented something of a false start for the politicians.

The barons had spent much blood and treasure to bring John to Runnymede. By a great feat of arms they had put John into a position where he had no choice but to accede to their demands and seal Magna Carta; but John had already put himself in a position where he lacked the power validly to do so. *Nemo dat quod non habet* – no one can give something that they do not have. John had given the crown to Innocent and had received it back as a vassal. The crown was not his to do with as he pleased. The crown belonged to Innocent and only Innocent could agree to limit the powers of the crown. John might as well have sent his bottle-washer to seal Magna Carta; no one in England had the power to agree what the document purported to do. All John needed to do was run crying to the Pope (as he duly did) and the Pope would annul Magna Carta (as, again, duly happened). From the point of view of feudal law John had done the barons up like kippers. If the force of law was important to them (and if it were not then why bother with Magna Carta in the first place?) then they would have to accept that John was not a competent signatory and that the document had no legal validity.

Here was the significance of the Golden Bull. How could this be the Pope's business? What possible right could Innocent have to determine these matters? Everything dealt with in Magna Carta, from the rights of the City of London to the right to hunt in certain forests, to the right to keep the King within the law, were legitimate subjects for discussion and determination in England. As a result of the Golden Bull, however, such discussions could only meaningfully take place in Rome. John's submission to the Pope meant that John's subjects lost the ability legally to determine English politics in England. Whatever Magna Carta's political significance, it was, from a legal point of view, worthless. Or rather, it would be worthless for as long as England was ruled by a papal nominee.

The barons had originally gone to war with John in his capacity as King of England. Now they would wage war against him in his capacity as a papal vassal. The aim would be to remove a king who was dependent upon the Pope and establish one who could validly agree to Magna Carta and who could then be expected to rule in accordance with it. This was more than rebellion; it was revolution. It was, however, a revolution with an unusual twist. The king whom the barons wanted to anoint was Louis, son and heir to Philip of France.

The prospect of Louis of England was not just pie in the sky. The barons invited him to land in England at the head of a French army. They then welcomed him into London and proclaimed him King at St Paul's Cathedral. Various nobles (including Alexander II, King of Scots) did homage to Prince Louis as King of England. Louis soon had much of the country in his hands. Had this fighting continued it must be thought likely that Prince Louis would have prevailed. Unhappily for Louis, the fighting was not to continue for long. There was only one way in which John could unite England's warring factions and, on 19 October 1216, he did just that. He died.

On John's death his young son, Henry, emerged as a possible monarch. Those who had been loyal to John naturally took up Henry's cause. Many of the rebel barons also thought that a young, pliable, English Henry was a safer bet than Prince Louis and they shifted their allegiance accordingly. Prince Louis fought on for a year but, eventually, he was forced out and in the Treaty of Lambeth he acknowledged that he had never been the rightful King of England. Henry III was recognised as monarch, Magna Carta was reissued in Henry's name (no appeal to the Pope was made and no independent papal denunciation appeared) and a long and eventful reign ensued.

The concept of a thousand years of English sovereignty now looks rather sickly. Following the Golden Bull, England was not a sovereign country and our ultimate master was Innocent III. This had, as we have seen, a major impact on Magna Carta, delaying the date on which it came into force until 1217 when it was reissued by Henry III.

What happened to the Golden Bull? Is it still in force? Are we now under the ultimate legal power of Pope Francis? Unsurprisingly, I would argue not. Henry III indulged a fantasy that the Golden Bull was still intact but this bore no relation to the political reality in the England over which he reigned. The barons had fought a revolutionary war against Innocent III (albeit waged against Innocent's vassal). They recognised that John had validly conveyed ultimate sovereignty to Innocent and they acknowledged that Innocent had legally appointed John King. The barons were faced with a political reality and they set out to alter this reality by military force. It may sound odd to speak of the barons fighting in the English Revolution against Rome, but what else can it have been? The barons wanted to depose England's lawful sovereign and replace his appointee with their own man. That can only be a revolution. Had the barons succeeded before John's death, they would have made Louis King of England and, though we are now trespassing into counter-factual history, it is perfectly possible that they could have kept him there. Fortunately, a neater solution was available and they selected Henry III. True, Henry was crowned by the Papal Legate but there was little question that he reigned only with baronial consent. Nor did the Pope try to claim either that Henry's reissue of Magna Carta breached feudal duties to an overlord or that Henry was liable to pay any of the tribute money set out under the Golden Bull.

This interpretation of history makes the Magna Carta barons heroes on two counts: firstly as champions of English liberties against the power of the monarch, and secondly as champions of England's sovereignty against a papal overlord.

The sorry story of John, the Pope and the Golden Bull shows that our sovereignty has not been intact for a thousand years and proves that there is rather more to the history of England's relationship with Europe than meets the eye. Our imagined idea of our national history does not recall that John's reign saw us bloodlessly conquered by an Italian Pope. Yet this is worth remembering. Our brief period of papal rule shows us that our sovereignty has been less durable than we have come to believe. The Barons' Revolution, however, shows us the tenacity with which we have been prepared to fight to reclaim that sovereignty should it be lost. The barons and those who fought with them battled to bring English sovereignty back to English territory. That is as noble a cause as Magna Carta and they deserve to be remembered for both.

Bloody Mary and the Spanish Match

England stood on the brink. Europe's most powerful country had massed a mighty fleet and despatched it northwards. It was 1588 and the Spanish Armada was at sea.

Drake was summoned from the bowling green and the sailors were called to their ships. The militia, too, was mustered. Determination to resist the Spaniards swept the land. Spanish victory would see the repression of Protestantism and the establishment of a puppet monarch. London would have to take its instructions from Madrid. The English needed no convincing of the severity of the stakes; they had seen it all before.

It had only been a few decades since England had last risen to defend itself from Spain. The crucial difference was that, in the case of the Spanish Armada, the monarch was where she should have been: at Tilbury with her soldiers, leading the defence. In the 1550s it had been a different story. The nation had been ready to fight the Spanish but the Queen had preferred to welcome them. Philip of Spain may have been England's aspirant invader in 1588 but he had been her King between 1554 and 1558. Philip had married Elizabeth's half-sister and predecessor, Mary I. As such he had become King and built himself a place of influence within the English state. During Philip's time as King of England, Catholicism was re-imposed, Protestants were burnt at the stake and English soldiers were killed serving Spanish foreign policy.

The memory of all this helped embolden the hearts of our defenders in 1588; but we have rather forgotten it since. We should remember. The struggle against Spain in the 1550s was at least as important as the battle of 1588 and it has much to teach us about the safeguarding of sovereignty. In the 1550s, perhaps remembering John and the

Golden Bull[2], we realised how easily independence could be lost and we took active steps to defend our freedom. This meant that unlike the Golden Bull, which was largely unopposed at the time and which was only challenged years after its conclusion, the marriage between Mary and Philip was fiercely resisted well in advance.

First there was a political effort to dissuade Mary from the marriage, next there was armed rebellion and finally there was a resort to law and an effort to secure English liberty by treaty and Act of Parliament. The people behind these efforts were just as much champions of England's sovereignty as their later colleagues in Drake's fleet. In this chapter we will see how they prosecuted their campaigns and we will see how their efforts fared. We will also, alas, see why they failed and, importantly, we will see what lessons we can learn from their experiences.

Before examining these questions, however, we must first try to understand Mary's point of view. Why was the Queen so desperate to snub her subjects and inflict a Spanish king on her realm?

There is an inevitable degree of speculation involved when trying to judge the motivations of those who died centuries ago, but three factors seem to be significant. The first is the nature of her parents' marriage and of her early life. The second is the bitter circumstances surrounding the annulment[3]of her parents' marriage. The third is the contested nature of her own succession. All of these tended to turn her away from England and towards Spain. We shall examine each in turn.

Mary's parents' marriage, like that of many royal marriages in the sixteenth century, was conditioned by foreign policy. Prince Henry,

---

[2] Which we saw in Chapter 1.

[3] Contrary to the rhyme that we all learnt at school, Henry and Catherine did not divorce; their marriage was annulled. Whether "Annulled, beheaded died..." will ever catch on is another question.

later Henry VIII, and Catherine of Aragon were wed to serve the needs of their respective countries. In Henry's case the decision was made by his father, Henry VII.

Henry VII headed a new dynasty. His claim to the throne rested more on conquest than on royal descent. The Wars of the Roses had been a turbulent and traumatic time. Henry's victory at the Battle of Bosworth had brought this war to a close but the security of his rule was far from certain. His first task was to steady his realm. This he did with consummate success. Though himself a Lancastrian, he married Elizabeth of York and thereby managed to unite the warring blooms in the Tudor Rose that appears on many of our 20p coins. He brought the barons to heel with the Courts of Star Chamber and High Commission. He managed the nation's finances with care and aplomb, leaving a fortune for Henry VIII to spend on wars against the French. An important part of his strategy was to forge an alliance with one of Europe's newest and greatest powers.

The union of Aragon and Castile had added the Kingdom of Spain to the map of Europe. The wealth and might of this new country made them a force to be reckoned with and their endorsement would help consolidate Henry's position. In exchange Henry could offer support in Spain's likely conflict with France. The terms of the alliance were written up in the Treaty of Medina del Campo. The pact was to be sealed by the marriage of Henry's heir, Prince Arthur to the Spanish Princess, Catherine of Aragon. In the end the bulk of the treaty rather fell by the wayside but the marriage plan endured and Arthur and Catherine were wed in November 1501. Their marriage did not long outlast their honeymoon as Arthur died in early 1502. This death, however, did not alter the political significance of a marital alliance between the thrones of England and Spain. The consensus in both countries was that it made sense for Catherine to be married to England's future king; Arthur was gone so Catherine should marry Prince Henry.

The obvious difficulty with that idea was that Henry was Catherine's brother-in-law and Holy Scripture puts such a marriage out of bounds. This could be overcome only if Arthur and Catherine's marriage had not been consummated and if the Pope gave a dispensation to approve the new match. Arthur, clearly, was not available for comment but Catherine swore that there had been no consummation. Whether or not this was true we will never know (though the idea that a pair of teenaged newlyweds would be capable of five months of chastity sounds a little, well, "bonkers"). In any case Catherine maintained that she had never been truly married to Arthur and that she was therefore free to contract a marriage with Henry. Pope Julius II, having been given the word of a princess, was prepared to accept Catherine's story at face value and provided the necessary dispensation. Henry and Catherine were to be wed. Mary would be the product of that union. She may have been an English princess but she was also a daughter of Spain and she would never forget that her parents' marriage had been engineered, at least in part, to secure the position of England's king. The idea of using Spanish power to uphold the English monarchy was almost literally in her DNA. Her early experiences would bring this idea into sharp and personal focus.

It is true that, in not being a boy, Mary began life as a disappointment to her father but this disappointment was not as acute as it would later be. Catherine, after all, was still reasonably young and might yet bear Henry a son. Moreover, in the meantime, Henry now had a useful bargaining chip in Europe's game of great power politics. The King was keen to make use of this opportunity.

Mary's first fiancé was Francis, heir to the King of France. Becoming engaged is usually an important milestone in a person's life but, as Mary was only two years old at the time, it is unlikely that she was all that interested. This proposed French match lasted only three years before being broken off. Much more important was her betrothal to Charles V, Holy Roman Emperor. Charles was a member of the Spanish royal family and was Mary's cousin on her mother's side. He was also 22 years old while Mary was only six so, even allowing for the sexual mores of the sixteenth century, it would be some years before the engagement could become a marriage. In fact, Charles and Henry would later think better of the deal and call things off. Nevertheless, for many of her formative years, Mary grew up in the expectation that she would become a Spanish princess and a European empress. She was trained and educated for the role and she became comfortable with the prospect.

All this would have given Mary an attitude to patriotism that was almost unique to royal wives and prospective royal wives. As Henry VIII's daughter we can assume that she had a high regard for England but she expected that the bulk of her life would be spent elsewhere and that she would, at some point, have to transfer her loyalty to another king and to a different country. Almost from birth she was conditioned to view patriotism as a changeable dichotomy; her future subjects saw it as a unity. Though no one could have known it at the time, the seeds of trouble were being liberally sown. What happened next would ensure that these seeds would grow into a bumper crop. Mary's privileged life was about to be turned upside down. She would come to see England as a hostile place, teeming with enemies, and, as her father turned her away, she would cleave ever more strongly to her mother and, indirectly, to Spain. The cause of the trouble was that Henry wanted a son and Catherine had become a problem.

Henry was profoundly mindful of his duty to the succession. He needed a male heir to show that the Tudor dynasty had a future. Catherine had left child-bearing age behind her but none of her sons had survived infancy. The Queen therefore moved from being Henry's hope for the future to being a barrier to his ambitions. This would probably have been enough to seal Catherine's fate. There was, however, a second threat to her position: another woman.

If cold-blooded calculation regarding the need for dynastic security had made Henry consider ditching Catherine, hot-blooded lust clinched the decision. Henry seems to have fallen pretty hard for Anne Boleyn. Anne was a highly regarded and very attractive young lady. Unkind myth has damned her reputation. We may, however, ignore many of the more fanciful stories, as many only appeared years after her fall from grace. We may fairly assume, for instance, that had she really been the tri-breasted nymphomaniac of legend, this might just possibly have merited some mention in contemporary records. In fact, far from being a voracious sexual predator, Anne's early dealings with Henry were characterised more by restraint than by enthusiasm. While her sister, Mary Boleyn, had rushed eagerly into the role of royal mistress, Anne stood aloof. Henry courted and Anne rebuffed. Henry was not used to rejection– and it seems to have helped secure Anne's position. The more he could not have her, the more ardently he wanted her.

All of this spelt the end of Catherine's time as Queen of England. This much was clear: Catherine would be out and Anne would be in. How this would come about was rather less obvious. The path eventually taken would have far-reaching constitutional implications, would sever Henry's realm from continental Christendom and, looked at from the point of view of the pious, would free or damn every soul in England. At the outset, however, few would have predicted any of this. Henry just wanted to ditch his wife. Mary would have to stand and watch as this happened. The spectacle would make for disagreeable viewing. Henry's opening gambit had brutal implications.

The King did not have to look particularly hard for grounds on which to end the marriage. After all, even before the wedding, many had said that the marriage was illegal. Back then, of course, Henry had taken the opposite view; now he changed his mind. The King now claimed that Arthur and Catherine had indeed consummated their marriage. If that were so, Julius II's dispensation would have been granted on a false premise and was of no effect. Henry and Catherine, therefore, had never been truly married. The King petitioned the Pope to declare his marriage void.

Catherine and Mary must have been appalled. Henry was calling Catherine a liar. More than that, he was claiming that she had been living with him not as a wife but as a whore. In Mary's case, the new analysis meant that, far from being a royal princess and heiress to the throne, she was a mere bastard. Catherine and Mary lacked the strength to fight the King themselves. If they were to have any hope of reprieve they would need the help of powerful allies. They found little support in England and had to look abroad.

By this time, Clement VII was on St Peter's throne and it was he who considered Henry's petition. The King can hardly have been optimistic. Clement was not going to scour the Bible or review the writings of the Church Fathers. His Holiness would not engage in complicated theological examination nor spend anguished hours seeking guidance in prayer. Rome was under the control of Charles V (the same Holy Roman Emperor whom we have already met as Catherine's nephew and Mary's one-time betrothed). Clement asked Charles what to do and Charles instructed the Pope to declare the marriage valid.

From Mary's point of view, the lesson was clear. She could not rely on her father nor on England; if she was to look for support from anywhere, it would be from Spain. This was a lesson that she would not forget.

In this case, however, even Spanish support would not be enough. Henry was not to be so easily stopped. Ideally he would have liked to have had the annulment and to have had it from the Roman

Catholic Church but, if push came to shove, his priority was the annulment and if the only way he could get that was by abandoning the Church of Rome then so be it.

It must have been devastating for Mary to see the lengths to which her father would go to excise her and her mother from his life.

Detaching England from Roman Catholicism was a momentous step and even a monarch as powerful as Henry could not hope to achieve it in a single bound. England was a Catholic country. Catholic bishops sat in England's Parliament and Catholic monasteries owned vast chunks of English land. The people of England were baptised, married and buried according to the rites of the Catholic Church. Scrapping all that, and more besides, would be no easy matter.

Henry also had power politics to consider. He was no revolutionary. The Pope was an established power and Henry did not like to see established powers challenged. Indeed, earlier in his reign the King had written *The Defence of the Seven Sacraments* championing Roman Catholic orthodoxy against the attacks of protestant reformers; he had been rewarded with the title *Fidei Defensor* for his efforts. For Henry to turn from arch Catholic game keeping to ardent Protestant poaching would represent no small career change. It could not be accomplished overnight; something more gradual was called for.

Henry would tread the path away from Rome with a series of small steps. He would repatriate powers gradually and he would avoid a direct conflict with the Papacy until the legal basis of the Reformation was largely complete.

The early measures were relatively uncontroversial. First to go was the right of appeal to Rome; no longer could English justice be overridden by Roman caprice. Next it became illegal to publish papal instructions and the King claimed the right of veto over ecclesiastical legislation. The Pope excommunicated Henry but this was an empty gesture. Henry had already demonstrated such contempt for the Holy See that his reputation could not be hurt by them returning his scorn. The King pressed on. He took the power to nominate bishops and then, to complete the break with Rome, he had Parliament pass the Supremacy Act and the Treason Act. The former declared that Henry was "the only supreme Head on Earth of the Church of England" and the latter made it treason to deny the validity of the former. That was that. England had left the Roman Catholic Church.

It is worth reflecting for a moment on what this meant. For many individuals it will have meant very little. The Church (with the exception of the monasteries) carried on much as before but with Henry taking the place of the Pope. Nor did the Reformation enhance the day-to-day freedom of the average Englishman. From the point of view of high politics, however, it was an event of seismic importance: the repudiation of Rome freed the English constitution from the spectre of formal outside control. No longer would a foreign power appoint our great officials or overrule our courts. It was now the case, moreover, that all elements of ultimate legal authority sat in London, and were, therefore, within the scope of rebellion. If England staged a popular revolt against the Pope, His Holiness could afford to ignore it; if England staged a popular revolt against the King, His Grace could not. It is unusual that a political reform empowers both a dictator and his people but the break with Rome did just that. Henry was made master of his subjects' souls but, in the final analysis, the people of England were made more fully masters of their political fate. The English Reformation made a truer reality of English liberty. However, the theological and political ramifications are but parts of the story. Also important is the impact on one scared young woman.

Mary's family life had been destroyed. She and her mother had suffered the bitterest humiliations. They now had to accept radically downgraded status and to watch as Anne Boleyn triumphed at court. They can only have taken cold comfort in Anne's subsequent failure and beheading after she only managed to produce a daughter (the future Elizabeth I).

The last few years of her father's reign saw Mary enjoy some sort of recovery. She was allowed to attend court and sometimes even acted as Henry's official hostess (during those periods when Henry was "between wives"). Nevertheless, she remained legally a bastard and her position never began to equate to what it had been before her parents' annulment. Nor would things get any better when Henry died.

Edward VI was as emphatically Protestant as Mary was fervently Roman Catholic and, on the whole, Mary found his reign a trying time. She knew, however, that her brother's reign might be short. Edward was young and sickly. While it was possible that he might enjoy a long life and that he might father a large collection of Protestant heirs, this did not look particularly likely. Mary had no realistic hope of displacing Edward VI but she could now look to a possible improvement in her prospects. If Edward died young and left no children, Mary might have a shot at taking the throne. Edward, and his advisers, were no less aware of this possibility than Mary had been and they did all they could to shut her out. Edward decreed that, should he die before he had children, the crown should go to his distant (but Protestant) cousin, Lady Jane Grey.

Lady Jane was not well-known in England but she had powerful friends. Only days before she was named Edward's heir she had married Guildford Dudley. Dudley's father was the Duke of Northumberland, Lord Protector of England. On Edward's death, Northumberland moved quickly to secure his daughter-in-law's position. On 10 June 1553, Jane was proclaimed Queen of England. Her position looked unassailable. The chief powers of the land were at her disposal. Northumberland controlled London and with it the seat of Government and the Treasury. The English Army and the Royal Navy likewise took their orders from the former Lord Protector.

Mary, by contrast, was in East Anglia with a few loyal retainers but no soldiers and no money. True to form, Mary tried to enlist help from abroad. This time her foreign friends let her down. They looked at the relative strengths of Jane and of Mary and concluded that the Marian cause was lost. They were wrong.

It was only on a superficial analysis that Jane had the upper hand. She had no basis of support amongst the people. Monarchy needs more than legal force if it is to have political reality. There has to be a willing bond between crown and country. A modern monarchy is in trouble if people stop wanting to buy Royal Wedding mugs and Royal Christening tea towels. A similar test in the sixteenth century was the volume at which people shouted "God save the Queen" when a new reign began. In Jane's case the decibel level was worryingly low. Mary, by contrast, had a certain popularity. Her Catholic faith was unhelpful but she was her father's daughter and nearest surviving heir, and that was enough for most Englishmen.

Slowly but surely, the gentry of East Anglia began to swing behind Mary and, gradually, an army began to form. Northumberland set off to meet this threat and, in his absence, the people of London began to agitate for Mary. The members of the Privy Council were not themselves great allies of Jane and they, too, swung behind Mary. On 20th June, the proclamation ceremony was repeated – with two important changes. The first was that, instead of proclaiming the accession of Jane, the herald announced the succession of Mary. The second difference was that the silent crowds were replaced by a cheering populace. Not long afterwards, Mary would enter the capital in triumph and take possession of the state. The reign of the Nine Day Queen was over.

The new Queen had been brought to the throne by the people of England. Spain had not lifted a finger to help her. On the other hand, it had seemed a damned close-run thing. Had the people of East Anglia been more timid she might never have won the early support that had made her a viable candidate. Moreover, the English had been quite happy to stand by and watch as she was disgraced by her father and brother. If Mary had been greater-hearted (and more politically astute) she might have put this behind her and determined to deepen her support among the people by ruling in accordance with their interests and wishes. Alas, this seems not to have entered her mind. Her accession was the last issue of note on which Mary and her subjects were to see eye to eye and the first difference in opinion was not long in coming. The issue was that of the Queen's marriage.

An English queen regnant was a new invention and, in the sexist world that was sixteenth-century England, it was a troubling one. There was a widespread view that Mary would not be able to bear the burdens of monarchy alone and that she would soon need a husband with whom to share them. The problem was that this would not be like a king marrying a lady and making her his queen. A queen consort did not automatically acquire any legal power. The husband of a queen regnant very likely would. After all, did not a wife promise to obey her husband? If the Queen of England promised to obey her husband would that not make her husband England's de facto ruler? Like all the kingdoms of medieval Europe, England lived under the shadow of the fact that it could be conquered on the battlefield; now an additional threat arose. England could be conquered through the marriage bed. Given this, the people of England had an understandable interest in who this husband would be and they had one criterion of overriding importance: he should be English. Queen Mary disagreed.

As the Queen began to cast her eyes over the courts of Europe, looking for a literal Prince Charming, the courts of Europe looked straight back at her. They could see that England was up for grabs. The Spanish leapt into action.

The Holy Roman Emperor had taken a keen interest in the Queen's marital prospects. Partly, no doubt, this was the result of genuine cousinly affection and of a sincere concern that the people of England should benefit from a secure dynasty attached to the True Faith. However, the Emperor also had several baser motives. Spain was at war with France and English troops might tip the balance in Spain's favour. England's traditional anti-French antipathy had not been enough to tempt them to fight but if their Queen were married to a senior member of the Spanish royal family, how could she, or her people, stand aloof? Spain wanted Mary to marry the Emperor's son and heir, Prince Philip. Mary may not have shared their reasoning but she reached the same conclusion. She would rather have a foreigner as her husband than an Englishman and she would prefer a Spaniard most of all. Philip was the outstanding candidate.

Looking at her childhood, at her adolescence and at the circumstances surrounding her accession it is not hard to understand why. Her early years had led her to grow comfortable with the idea of marriage to a foreign (particularly a Spanish) prince. She had her mother's memory and her own mistreatment to avenge, and an alliance with Catholic Spain would go some way towards achieving that. Finally, Mary would have been acutely conscious that her support in England had almost never been enough. It had not stopped her father from disinheriting her and it had not stopped her brother from naming a distant cousin as his heir in place of her. It was true she had received sufficient support to establish herself on the throne, but this support had not been strong enough to give her an undisputed succession. Elizabeth I would famously place her security in the love of her people; Mary was not confident enough for that. She would rely on the arms of a foreign power. It is easy to see why some of England's leaders saw the idea of Mary marrying a foreign prince as being tantamount to an alliance between Mary and an overseas kingdom against the interests and liberties of the people of England: on one level, that was exactly what it was.

The stage was set for conflict but would the supporters of an English marriage be able to agree on a suitable candidate? In other circumstances this question could well have provoked disagreement and even civil war. However, the rampant and internecine slaughter of the Wars of the Roses had eliminated many noble houses and impoverished many of those which survived. This meant that potential suitors were fewer on the ground than might otherwise have been the case. Moreover, the prospect of a foreign alternative concentrated domestic minds. English opinion coalesced around Edward Courtenay, Earl of Devon.

Courtenay was a great-grandson of Edward IV and thus had royal blood in his veins. He had not played a particularly significant role in previous reigns because his father had been executed for plotting with Catholics under Henry VIII and both Henry and his son took the view that Courtenay was best left in the Tower of London. Mary's accession brought his release and he seemed to enjoy some royal favour when at liberty. Courtenay was the hope of those who favoured an English marriage.

During 1553 both sides pressed their claims. Renard, the Emperor's ambassador in England, presented his master's case with great force. He played on Mary's Catholicism, her loyalty to her late mother and the support that Spanish money could give her should she ever face difficulties from her Protestant subjects.

Mary's English counsellors advised her to marry Courtenay. They explained the threats to England's sovereignty. England, they said, would become embroiled in Spain's wars. They pointed out that, as heir to the wealthiest throne in Europe, Philip would be well-placed to exploit his position in England and to become the foremost power in the land. Mary's advisers also expressed their fear that, if the royal couple had children, then the monarchies of England and Spain could be united not only in one marriage but in one person. The Queen's counsellors explained that Spain, Europe's sole superpower, would be the more appealing kingdom and that England would be relegated to second-class status. These were powerful arguments, but they left Mary unmoved. The Queen announced her intention to marry Philip.

This news hit England like a match hitting a tinder box. The prospect of a Catholic king horrified the populace. The groans of Spain's persecuted Protestants had long been heard in England and they offered grim testimony of the nature of Catholic rule. People felt sure that Philip's coronation would bring those nightmares to England. The Spanish Inquisition would set up branch offices throughout the land. Torture would be commonplace, martyrs numerous and fear universal. St George himself seemed to weep for England. There was only one way in which this could be avoided. Mary would have to be denied her husband and Philip's reign would have to be ended before it could begin; it was time for a pre-emptive revolution.

Sir Thomas Wyatt, an associate of Edward Courtenay and of those others who had first pressed for an English marriage, took the lead and organised a rebellion. Wyatt raised his standard in Kent, rallied several thousand men and marched on Rochester. Mary sent her troops to Rochester hoping that they would oust Wyatt and bring the rebellion to an end. She was to be disappointed. On arrival, faced with the prospect of fighting fellow English Protestants and risking life and limb to install a foreigner as king, Mary's soldiers lost heart. Some deserted but many stayed and joined the rebels. Emboldened, Wyatt headed for London. He was soon encamped in Hyde Park.

London braced itself for civil war. Thousands of rebels had massed in the centre of London. They had won defectors from Mary's own army. Mary however, still had loyal troops and these troops were well armed, well trained, well disciplined and well led. She could also rely on natural suspicion of rebellion and the associated disorder. While some Londoners did join Wyatt, most focussed on ensuring that they would be able to defend their own property in the event of rioting.

Wyatt led his men through the city, along Fleet Street and up to Ludgate. There they were met by the Queen's canon. Wyatt could see that, given the narrowness of Fleet Street, the large size of his band would count for little if they pressed on. He ordered an about-face. This was an inevitably chaotic and dispiriting performance and, just as the rebels were trying to put themselves back together, more of Mary's soldiers were advancing on their position. Battle broke out at Temple Bar. Englishmen fought and killed Englishmen in the heart of their capital city. Mary's proposed marriage was already costing the nation dear. In the end Mary's soldiers prevailed. The rebellion was crushed and Wyatt was executed. England's attempt to resist the Spanish match by force had failed. Mary would wed Philip. However, even though the marriage itself had become inevitable, all was not lost. The *nature* of the marriage was still uncertain.

Those who had opposed the marriage in council and on the battlefield had done so because of a fear that the husband of a queen regnant would acquire royal authority. As the marriage approached, more careful thought was given to this fear and some began to see a ray of hope. After all, there had never before been an English queen regnant so the legal status of such a queen's husband had not been properly considered, much less decided. This was uncharted constitutional territory; the rules had yet to be written. Perhaps English law could be drafted in such a way that a queen regnant's husband enjoyed no more legal power than a king's queen consort? Could a lawyer succeed where the soldiers had failed? What was needed was a man of learning, trusted by the Queen but loyal to England, who could draw up terms for the marriage by which Mary could give her hand to Philip but keep her kingdom to herself: step forward Stephen Gardiner.

Gardiner was one of that company of able men who, unfavoured by the blessings of noble birth or inherited wealth, was able to rise from humble beginnings to national prominence due to the combination of academic ability and a career in the Church.

It was Gardiner who was charged with negotiating the marriage treaty between England and Spain. His first concern was to protect England's sovereignty. Gardiner's position had been greatly strengthened by Wyatt's rebellion. Though a failure, this revolt had shown Mary and Philip that they could not have their way over the marriage without some considerable compromise on their part. Gardiner played this hand to its fullest strength. Parchment at the ready and quill in his hand, Gardiner sat down in his study and fought for England's freedom.

He was determined to safeguard our political independence. He threw his heart and soul into drafting a collection of legal documents designed to prevent Philip becoming king in more than name. The Spanish match, if Gardiner had his way, would not become a Spanish takeover. The centrepiece of Gardiner's efforts was an Act of Parliament – the Act for the Marriage of Queen Mary to Philip of Spain 1554. The best way to understand the Act is to understand Gardiner's thinking. He wanted to puzzle out all of Philips' hopes and plans; and then, having puzzled them out, he wanted to knacker them.

Philip's chief hope would be that Philip would become King of England in his own right and with a greater authority than that enjoyed by his wife. Gardiner's job was to make sure that did not happen. He therefore drafted the Marriage Act so that it merely accorded Philip "the style, honour and kingly name of the realms and dominions unto the said most noble queen appertaining". This gives him the title but, to the eyes of a medieval lawyer, the absence of any reference to "kingly power" would have been glaring. The fact that Philip would not enjoy kingly power is made even clearer in the following clauses when his role as Mary's husband is set out.

The Act says that Philip is to "aid" the Queen in "the happy administration of her Grace's realms and dominions". Far from ruling a kingdom he was reduced to assisting his wife and, as if that were not enough, the Act presses on to say that "the rights, laws, privileges and customs of the same realms and dominions [i.e. England]" would be "preserved and maintained". Not only would there not be Spanish government, there would not even be any Spanish-style reforms. So much for Philip.

Gardiner, however, saw that even if there were a legal bar on Philip's own influence, there was a risk that he might, under the guise of "aiding" his wife, appoint some of his Spanish friends to Government posts. If that was indeed Philip's hope, Gardiner was waiting for him. According to the Act, Philip will "permit and suffer the said most gracious queen his wife, to have the whole disposition of all the benefices and offices...of the said realms and dominions". Gardiner was a clever man and saw that this might leave scope for Philip to pressure Mary to appoint some of his supporters so he widened the prohibition by insisting that "the benefices and offices" of England may only be "bestowed upon such as shall be naturally born in the same". No jobs for the Spanish boys.

Even without the prospect of official Government jobs, Philip would doubtless bring some Spanish courtiers with him and, indirectly, these courtiers could pose a threat so it was agreed that Philip "shall bring none in his retinue, nor have none with him that will do any displeasure or wrong to the subjects of [England]; and if they do, he shall take order to correct them with condign punishment and see them expelled his court". For good measure Gardiner added that "all the matters of the said realms and dominions shall be treated and maintained in the same tongues wherein of old they have wont to be treated, and by the natural born of the same realms". English political debates would not take place in the Spanish language. Gardiner had set the terms of entry to the Government of England. And Philip was outside.

Medieval monarchy, however, was not just about governing; it was also about possessing. Some might think that, in marrying Mary, Philip might acquire legal ownership over her property. Whatever the rights and wrongs of that view, the Act sets out important restrictions on what Philip could do with any such property: Philip "shall not bear or carry over out of [England], the jewels and precious things of estimation, neither shall he alienate or do away any whit of the appurtenances of the said realm of England, or suffer any part of them to be usurped by his subjects or any other". Philip was further obliged not to allow "any ship, guns, ordnances whatsoever of war or defence to be removed or conveyed out of [England]". What was England's had to stay in England.

Of course, marriage was ordained for the procreation of children and here there were some tricky issues to be dealt with. Philip already had children. He already had an heir. If Philip became King of England, would his son become heir to that throne as well? Not if Gardiner had anything to do with it. The Act provides that "as touching the right of the mother's inheritance in the realm of England...the children...that shall be born of this matrimony shall succeed in them, according to the laws, statutes and customs of the same". The important point is that the children have to be born of "this matrimony" so there is nothing for Philip's existing children (though they are obviously left with their own inheritances from Philip).

The fact that Philip already had children meant that a union of the crowns was unlikely but, with his keen eye to all eventualities, Gardiner saw that it was not impossible. If Philip's existing children died and Mary and Philip themselves had a son, that prince could become King of Spain as well as of England. Such a monarch might well wish to subordinate England's interest to Spain's. Gardiner was ready with a suitable statutory provision: "If...the eldest son of this matrimony shall be admitted into the said right [i.e. to be King of Spain]...they shall leave to every of the said realms, lands and dominions [i.e. England] whole and entire their privileges, rights and customs, and the same realms and dominions shall administer and cause to be administered by the natural born of the same realms, dominions and lands, and in all things faithfully procure their utility and quiet, and shall rule and nourish them in good justice and peace, according to their statutes and customs". England and Spain might have the same King but he would have to reign very differently in his different realms. And what would happen if, as in fact did happen, the couple had no children and Mary predeceased Philip? In that case it was agreed that Philip "shall not challenge any right at all in the said kingdom, but without any impediment shall permit the succession thereof to come unto them to whom it shall belong and appertain by the right and laws of the said realm".

So much for the general questions of government, property and succession. There were also numerous more specific clauses. Charles[4] would want England to aid him in his war against France. Despite the sweeping restrictions set out elsewhere in the Act, Gardiner thought that this merited special attention and insisted on a clause to the effect that "the realm of England, by occasion of this matrimony, shall not directly or indirectly be entangled with the war that is between the most victorious lord the emperor, father unto [Philip], and Henry, the French king, but he the said lord Philip, as

[4] Philip's father.

much as shall lie in him, on the behalf of the said realm of England, shall see the peace between the said realms of France and England observed, and shall give no cause of any breach".

Wow.

Gardiner left no "i" undotted and no "t" uncrossed. Every legal avenue by which Spain might try to gain dominion over England was spotted. And blocked. The treaty stands as a pre-emptive declaration of independence. As a statement of liberty it could almost be mentioned in the same breath as Magna Carta and the 1688 Bill of Rights. As a piece of well-crafted constitutional law it is a model of its kind. A passion for England's freedom courses through the document. The treaty is politely crafted in the courtly language of its time but no amount of polish could conceal that its subtext could be expressed in three words: "get stuffed Philip". Why, one is forced to ask, did Spain bother to press on? The answer lies in the distinction between law and politics.

Gardiner's words are wonderful but laws are only as powerful as the will and ability to enforce them. Philip would have constant access to Mary and could build a powerful presence in Government. Gardiner wanted to make Philip a king in name but a queen consort in power. The problem should have been clear: queens consort had been very powerful indeed. Legally Philip's hands were bound but politically it was all to play for. As we will see, Philip did indeed act beyond the terms of the treaty and England suffered as a result. The first point related to religion.

Mary and Philip both wanted England to return to the Catholic faith but it was Philip who took the lead. It was Philip who wrote to the Pope about the sending of a senior Catholic prelate to England to serve as Archbishop of Canterbury, and it was Philip who led the efforts to have anti-Catholic legislation scrapped. Philip was also one of the prime movers in discussions about the status of the lands that had previously belonged to the monasteries. Philip clearly pressed his wife into bringing England back into the Roman Catholic Church. He may not personally have ordered the burnings of Protestants that were to give Bloody Mary her name but they certainly bear the stamp of his inspiration. Very possibly, Mary would have pursued a similar line had she been left to her own devices. The point, however, is that she was not left to her own devices. Philip was calling the shots. Nor was the King's influence restricted to domestic religious policy. He had wed Mary to gain control of the Royal Navy and the English army and he now wanted to put that control to use.

Philip wanted England to join Spain's war against France. This was clearly contrary to England's interests. Neither the English economy nor the English army was strong enough to face war. Such a war would, moreover, be illegal – the Marriage Act expressly forbade England from going to war with France on Spanish instructions. Philip, of course, cared nothing for England's concerns. Any English help would make Spain's task easier and, if providing such help proved ruinous to England, well, tough.

Mary's ministers could see that such a war would be a foolhardy enterprise and, initially, they opposed it. Philip's resolve was undimmed. The King and Queen set about bribing, threatening and cajoling the ministers until, finally, they got their way. England, which had no quarrel with France and which had few resources with which to support an invasion, declared war on France. It was to prove a disaster.

As England's statesmen had feared, the English army could not cope with extensive operations in a foreign land. Our forces were soon on the back foot and, far from taking the offensive alongside their Spanish allies, were reduced to defending our sole remaining outpost in France: Calais.

English since the fourteenth century, Calais was a brilliant staging post for England's trade with the Continent. By the time of Mary's reign, the fact that Calais was in English hands had long been a running sore. Philip and Mary's declaration of war gave the French the excuse they needed. The French army fell upon Calais with devastating destructive power. Within days, the English garrison was overcome and surrendered. Calais had been lost.

This defeat was a painful one. Calais was a pale shadow of the Angevin Empire but its symbolic value was immense. For as long as we held Calais, we had claims to be a Continental power and could feel one up on the French. The capture of Calais represented a body blow to our national prestige. Mary felt the loss acutely, claiming that when she was dead the word "Calais" would be found engraved upon her heart.

This was what the Spanish match had brought us. It had provoked civil war, it had brought England back into an alien Church, it had led to hundreds being burnt at the stake and it had led us into a costly war. And Philip had only been King for four years.

People feared for the future. Mary and Philip seemed a diabolical pair and many assumed that they would continue to wash the land with English blood. The succession was a no less terrifying prospect. Any of Mary's children would be brought up under Philip's influence and taught to share his priorities. England would become a permanent Spanish lackey. We would be drawn ever more closely into the web of European politics but we would be the junior partner and would have to watch as our resources and interests were squandered in the pursuit of Spanish aims. Eventually, perhaps, an English rebellion or even revolution would bring power back from Madrid and restore it to London but, in any case, the next few decades looked bleak.

Until Mary's ill health intervened.

Mary died childless and the Spanish threat died with her. The Queen's death brought a nightmare to a close, saved thousands of lives and restored English liberty. Elizabeth I came to the throne and we had a patriot Queen whose love for England was beyond reproach. Philip, in an effort to take England back peacefully, promptly proposed to her new Queen. She turned him down but he would not take rejection well. The Spanish Armada would be the eventual result. It was England's triumph over this formidable fleet that would finally put paid to Spain's hopes of conquering England.

What can we learn from the Spanish Match? The first lesson is to be quick off the mark. England's political class had stood idly by as John had agreed the Golden Bull. It was not until years later that they realised the extent of what had happened. With the Spanish Match the threat was identified early and steps were taken. The nature of those steps (and their failure) shows us the second lesson: not to confuse law with politics.

This was the mistake made by Stephen Gardiner. While his work on Mary and Philip's marriage treaty earns him a place in the pantheon of English heroes (after all, noble failure has never prevented entry to that august assembly), he had tried to fight a political battle with legal weapons and, ultimately, he could never hope to prevail. Philip's political position was unassailable. He had peerless influence over England's lawful sovereign and he had the wealth and might of Spain with which to back himself up. Whatever the legal fetters on his power, his political authority was immense. The result of this was that, despite all Gardiner's efforts and in direct contravention of the text of his treaty, England was dragged into Spain's war against France. English blood, treasure and territory were sacrificed at the whim and for the sake of a foreign power. That was exactly what Gardiner, Wyatt and many of their countrymen wished to avoid.

The third point is that ruler and ruled do not always share interests. A damning verdict against Mary is that this blood, treasure and territory was a price that she was willing to pay to win the right to expect foreign help should her hold on the throne be shaken. There can be no more fundamental breach of a monarch's duty to his or her people.

Sadly we would have to learn the second lesson again when a sovereign with even less honour than John or Mary came to disgrace the English crown: Charles II. At least Mary's treachery was publicly announced. Charles made duplicitous agreements in the strictest secrecy. Worse even than that, Mary only sold us out to Spain; Charles betrayed us to the French.

Charles II and the Secret Treaty of Dover

The English have seldom rejoiced as heartily as they did on 29th May 1660. London, in particular, was *en fête*. Londoners filled the taverns and thronged the streets. There was music and laughter, celebration and song. The epicentre of activity was a procession led by a young man visiting London for the first time since 1649. The young man in question was Charles Stuart and his people were welcoming him home. The Republic had fallen, the King had returned to his capital – all was right with England. The English were looking forward to a brighter future but they were also putting an enthusiastic end to a dark chapter in their nation's history.

Cromwell's England had been an unhappy place. The Government had been directed by zealous Puritans who were completely out of step with their countrymen. The Cromwellians wanted to transform England into a godly nation; they soon found that the English were unpromising material. We wanted cakes and we wanted ale. We wanted to dance around maypoles in the summer and we wanted to celebrate Christmas in the winter. We were happy to go to church on Sunday (provided the clergy could meet reasonable standards of brevity in their sermons) but we wanted to go our own way for the rest of the week. This was the English way of life. It horrified the Puritans.

In a grim programme of repression, Cromwell and his colleagues tried to drain the country of joy. Merrymaking was forbidden and revelry was outlawed. When the people failed to fall into line, the military took direct control and the country was divided into regions each controlled by a Major-General. Little wonder that, when all this came to an end, the English erupted in celebration.

Charles was a fitting poster boy for the return of the good life. He revelled in pleasure and excess. Good food, fine wine and plentiful sex were the stuff of which his court was made. Happily he wanted his subjects to enjoy themselves too. Maypoles and Christmas were back and alehouses could go unmolested by state oppression – all of which could be relied upon to produce contented Englishmen. So much about the Restoration seemed to augur so well. The "merry monarch" seemed to be the man for the time and he might have made a name for himself as one of our greatest kings. It was not to be. Charles and his people may have been in tune on "merriment" but they were at odds when it came to politics. The English valued their liberty. Charles did not.

Like his father and his grandfather, Charles II was an absolutist. The freedoms of his subjects counted for little with him. He meant to be the undisputed master of his realm. Sadly for him, England was in no mood to play host to a tyrant. If Charles pressed the point then conflict was inevitable. Few knew better than Charles what this would mean.

Charles had spent much of his youth watching his father, Charles I, wage war against his people. He had seen his father invoke the Divine Right of Kings, dismiss Parliament and rule alone. He had also seen the chaos of the Civil War that had followed and he remembered that, having lost, his father had been executed for treason. The lesson that Charles took from this was not that it was unwise to try to establish a dictatorship but that it was unwise to establish a dictatorship *in the same way as his father had done.*

Charles I had been open about his manifesto. He made clear his belief that God had called him to Government and that it was his right and duty to rule as he saw fit, without any input from Parliament. It was this openness, in Charles II's view, that had been his father's undoing. If Charles I had taken a subtler approach he might have reached his goal in peace. Charles II resolved to wage war against his people too; he just resolved to do so covertly. His secret escapades would lead him to make clandestine deals with France that involved surrendering control of great swathes of foreign policy. In this chapter we will see Charles II take underhand diplomacy to new depths – but we will also see how Parliament brought the King to heel once they discovered his treachery. First, however, we must understand why Charles decided to turn his back on his people and cosy up to a foreign power.

Charles' difficulty was that he wanted to establish an absolute monarchy but that he was also strapped for cash. The King had various sources of income but none were particularly lucrative. By themselves they would allow the monarch to conduct the business of Government in a small and unobtrusive way. They were not enough to support an activist policy either at home or abroad. If Charles wanted to run a dictatorship he would have to increase his income.

The most obvious way forward was to call Parliament and ask it to vote for fresh taxation. What Charles wanted, however, was to free himself from Parliament, so it would have set a poor precedent to have gone cap in hand to the Commons. He would also have struggled to justify his request for additional resources. Parliament could hardly be expected to agree to fund the establishment of royal despotism. The King soon realised that the better prospects were outside England and that his best hopes lay with the King of France, Louis XIV.

Louis was related to Charles, was himself an absolute monarch and would be eager to have English support for his aggressive foreign policy. He also had cash to spend. But Louis would not be careless with his overseas aid. He would expect considerable bang for his buck. Louis' focus would be on the two areas that mattered most to him: religion and war. Charles would be happy to make big promises on both counts.

The first point was religion. Louis disapproved of Protestantism. It encouraged freethinking and it nurtured liberty; Louis was emphatically opposed to both. The French King was taking action to suppress Protestantism within France but he saw how difficult this would be while French Protestants could look abroad and see foreign countries living happily under reformed religion. Louis wanted to deprive his Protestant subjects of these tempting examples by bringing the Protestant nations back to the Roman Church. If Charles wanted Louis' money he would have to commit to rewinding the Reformation. Given the extent to which Protestantism was now entrenched in England, this would not be an easy business, and it was only the start. In addition to this spiritual pledge, Louis would want Charles' help on an earthly battlefield.

Louis was intent on war with Holland. The Dutch were protestant, rich and few in number. They also shared a border with France. All of this put Holland firmly in Louis' sights. If he could conquer Holland, Louis could have the glory of subjugating religious heretics, he could win a group of wealthy taxpayers and he could expand the territorial reach of his kingdom. The Dutch had everything he wanted. Alas, there was a problem – the Dutch also had powerful friends.

In 1668, the English, the Dutch and the Swedes had entered into the Triple Alliance. Despite the maritime rivalry that had twice led England and Holland into war, this was a popular alliance. The English recognised that the Dutch were both Protestant and anti-French and, as such, saw them as natural allies. The Triple Alliance scuppered Louis' hopes for Holland.

As long as the English and the Swedes stood alongside the Dutch, Louis' ambitions could not be realised. Louis therefore determined to break up the Triple Alliance.

In ordinary circumstances this would have been difficult. The Triple Alliance had been concluded in good faith between countries whose peoples shared many important affinities. If Louis was to bring the Triple Alliance to an end, he would need to persuade England or

Sweden (or both) to perform a dramatic volte-face. Under the Triple Alliance they were pledged to aid Holland should France invade; Louis would have to persuade them to stand aside or, ideally, to assist the French. Could Louis find an English or Swedish leader so unprincipled as to take his country down that path? Absolutely, for England was ruled by Charles II. Louis wanted Charles to abandon the Dutch and throw his lot in with France.

The basis of a bargain between Charles and Louis was grimly apparent. Louis' wish was for Charles to embrace Catholicism and join a French war against the Dutch. Charles would be willing to make the necessary promises – for a fee. Negotiations soon began in earnest.

Standard diplomatic routes were out of bounds. Charles could not trust his officials with these wicked arrangements. If anything, however, Charles would have regarded this as a bonus. The usual ambassadors would have been the younger sons of courtiers or able clerks keen to make names for themselves. The King would have found such emissaries woefully sub-scintillating. The surreptitious nature of this enterprise required go-betweens of an altogether different (and much more agreeable) stamp. The chief envoys were attractive young women who, under the sexist standards prevailing at the time, would not be suspected of diplomatic intrigue. Louise de Kérouaille was one such. A lady of great charm and beauty, she had been a lady-in-waiting at the French court. Louis took the view that she could best serve France between the sheets of England's royal bed. Louis had been looking for someone to influence the English King and persuade Charles to reach an agreement with Louis that favoured France rather more than it favoured England. Louis had judged Charles well; he did indeed find Louise irresistible.

By the summer of 1670, Charles was ready to agree one of the most shameful treaties in the history of English diplomacy. The Secret Treaty provided as follows:

> "The King of England will make a public profession of the Catholic faith, and will receive the sum of two millions of crowns, to aid him in this project, from the Most Christian King, in the course of the next six months...The two Kings will declare war against the United Provinces. The King of France will attack them by land, and will receive the help of 6000 men from England. The King of England will send 50 men-of-war to sea, and the King of France 30; the combined fleets will be under the Duke of York's command."[5]

We can see why Charles would have wanted to keep this treaty secret.

By signing up to these terms, Charles was agreeing to betray his allies, his faith and his people. He was also confirming that, in the end, there was no principle that counted so much with him as Stuart absolutism. The English people did not want a Catholic king, they did not want to abandon the Dutch and they did not want to aid the French. As the English king, these convictions should have mattered to Charles; they clearly did not.

Nor can there be any doubt as to whether Charles fully understood how unpopular these commitments would be. He was to receive two million crowns to "aid" him in his public profession of the Roman Catholic faith. This aid would be required because such a declaration would cause uproar in England and Charles would need money to fund the defence of his throne. The two million crowns was French money that the King of England would take to use against his own subjects. This sort of behaviour would have appalled even King John. It was a grotesque abandonment of sovereignty.

---

[5] http://archive.org/stream/madamelifeofhenr00adyjrich/madamelifeofhenr00adyjrich_djvu.txt

Not that this would have bothered Charles. He had cheerfully trousered socking great wodges of French loot. His mind was not troubled by sovereignty or national interest; it was far too busy with congenial thoughts of wine, of women and, thereafter, of absolute monarchy. Alas for Charles, reality was about to intervene. Louis asked Charles to keep his end of the bargain – and declare war on the Dutch.

This was more complicated than it seemed. Wars are expensive affairs and the French money was a secret. As far as Parliament and the English people were concerned, the King was in relatively straightened circumstances. They imagined that he could fund his court and the various expenses of civil administration, but few thought that he had the resources for a military campaign. If Charles suddenly announced that he had acquired serious quantities of cash and was in a position to wage war without recourse to Parliament it would, to say the least, raise some eyebrows.

People would wonder where exactly this money had come from, and it would not take them long to guess. They would not have needed a seventeenth-century WikiLeaks to crack this case. Two facts would have been immediately self-evident. The first was that the biggest winner from an English declaration of war against the Dutch would be the French King, and the second was that few people other than Louis were in a position to provide funds on the necessary scale. It would become clear that Charles had been bribed by Louis and that he had sold control of England's foreign policy to Paris. Regardless of the subsidies, therefore, Charles would have to find some access to ready money.

This was a problem in that, as we have seen, Charles' own resources were limited and he could not go to Parliament. He could have tried to raise funds by levying new taxes without parliamentary approval but he knew that to do so would be to provoke widespread rebellion. He could not obtain money by fair dealing. So he would cheat.

Charles was heavily in debt. The City of London had advanced large sums to Charles and, having frittered most of the money away, he was now struggling to pay in the interest (let alone to make capital repayments). Charles was not prepared to make savings in his spending on clothes, wine or women but he was happy to pay less to his bankers. Charles announced that there would be no repayment of capital or payment of interest on the bulk of the State's debt for the whole of 1673. The Great Stop of the Treasury, as it became known, gave Charles his money but proved ruinous for many banks and their customers. It also literally discredited the word of the English Crown. That word was to be further cheapened when Charles broke the Triple Alliance and declared war on Holland.

This declaration of war should have spelt the end for the Dutch. Attacked by England on the seas and by France overland, few bookies would have had Holland as the favourite to win this particular war. The bookies would have been reckoning, however, without William of Orange (whom we shall meet as William III in the next chapter).

By its very nature, the Dutch Republic had no hereditary head of state but the House of Orange had established a leading position and it was to the current head of that House that the eyes of the nation turned. They wanted William to lead their resistance to the invading French. Charles and Louis saw that William might make all the difference and offered to make him Prince of Holland if only he would join forces with them and accept that Holland should become a puppet state of France.

It is a sad comment on the Dover conspirators that they thought it would only be natural for a leader to betray his people if it would secure him a crown and win him a life of royal comfort. William was made of nobler stuff and scorned their offer. He injected a formidable vigour into the Dutch defence, opening the dykes and forcing the would-be conquerors to wade through sodden fields.

Just as William's bold leadership denied the French an easy victory on land, so the skill of his admirals proved too much for the English navy. Far from obtaining revenge for previous naval defeats at the hands of the Dutch, the course of the war was running against us.

The Third Anglo-Dutch War had always been unpopular in England but, had it gone well, that unpopularity might have been subsumed in the glow of victory. Alas, for Charles, that was not the way that things were working out. We were losing. And we were losing in some style. The costs of our losses soon outgrew Charles' ability to bear them. Hard-pressed himself, Louis could spare no money to prop up his English ally and, after the debacle of the Great Stop, no help could be expected from the City. That left only one option: Parliament.

The irony must have been bitter. Charles had agreed the Treaty of Dover in the hope that it would free him from the need to summon Parliament again; in fact, carrying out the Treaty's terms had put him in a situation where he was obliged to do just that. Nor would this be a quiescent Parliament. Charles had tried the patience of the nation. Had the war been won, had the French subsidies continued and had Charles made better use of those subsidies, this might not have mattered; he would have had the strength to defy the people and rule as a tyrant. But that was not the way things had worked out. The King had gambled and the King had lost. He would now have to face the consequences. Chief among those consequences was an angry Parliament. Its Members disliked Charles' Dutch war and were suspicious of his motives for engaging in it. They were determined to set policy on a more congenial course.

The Parliament that met in 1673 was one of the most ambitious in English history. They could see that Charles was his father's son (and, for that matter, his grandfather's grandson) in his loathing for Parliaments and determination to rule alone. It was failure in the Third Dutch War, rather than any pro-parliamentary inclination on Charles' part, that had brought them back to Westminster and many MPs will have seen this as a chance (potentially as the last chance) to assert their rights. They would do so with a vengeance. They would, in turn, take aim at the Royal Prerogative, at the King's choice of ministers, at foreign policy and at the succession. In all but the last they would enjoy considerable success.

The first step was to curtail the Royal Prerogative. Under the Prerogative, Charles had claimed the right to "dispense" with certain laws. Such a dispensation effectively abolished the law to which it referred. This aspect of the Prerogative put royal whim above the law of the land. That would have been bad enough, but one of Charles' main uses of his dispensing power had been to suspend various pieces of anti-Catholic legislation. This outraged England's Protestant Parliament. Its first step in 1673 was to undo much of the "dispensing" of the earlier part of Charles' reign. Parliament put the anti-Catholic laws firmly back onto the statute books. In doing so Parliament landed a body blow on royal prestige and power. The King had to sit there and take it. And there was more to come. Their early success had emboldened MPs and they moved on to consider Charles' ministers.

Parliament was concerned by a build-up of Roman Catholics in Government positions. MPs feared that England was at risk as long as policy was in the hands of non-Protestants. They therefore set out to remove Roman Catholics from the formal architecture of the English State. To do so Parliament passed the Test Act. This Act required the holders of public office to take the Holy Communion in accordance with Anglican rites and to denounce certain Catholic ideas such as transubstantiation. Roman Catholics could not satisfy these requirements and thus became ineligible for public office – even in the King's inner circle. Catholic influence had been curbed.

Parliament was on a roll. They had succeeded in restricting the use of the Royal Prerogative and they had forced undesirables out of the Government. Now they would turn their fire on another area of Government work that had, traditionally, been thought to belong solely to the King: foreign policy.

The House of Commons strongly urged the King to abandon the war against the Dutch. Without access to financial resources, Charles had no choice. He put the Treaty of Dover to one side and agreed terms with the Dutch.

Parliament was clearly in the driving seat. It had beaten the King, limited his powers and taken control of the major issues of the day and all without civil war. If the Treaty of Dover had seen the King yield control over the country to Louis, the House of Commons' reaction saw Parliament seize control over the King. The steps they took represented significant advances in the power of Parliament. Remarkably, however, they wanted to go still further. Their experiences with Charles had taught them much of Stuart ambition and duplicity. Charles was still an Anglican and yet he had a dangerous predilection for absolutism and Roman Catholicism. How much worse would things be if Charles' Roman Catholic brother became king? James, Duke of York terrified the Protestants.

Despite Charles II's extra-marital fecundity (fathering no fewer than 17 bastards), he had not produced a legitimate heir. This meant that James was heir to the throne.

James had been born and raised an Anglican. His first wife had been an Anglican and he had fathered two Anglican daughters. James' mother, however, had been a devout Roman Catholic and he had now converted to his mother's faith. His own Roman Catholicism was bad enough, but when he married the young and Catholic Mary of Modena it seemed that he might become the first in a long line of Catholic kings.

England's last Catholic monarch, Bloody Mary, was a poor ambassador for the brand and few welcomed the prospect of a return to the tyranny and executions with which her reign was associated. The Test Act had broached this issue. James had previously been Lord High Admiral but the Test Act forced him to resign. This led people to wonder how someone who was not permitted to be the country's senior admiral could still be eligible to succeed to the throne. Moves to bar James from the throne might have been very popular.

However, the English people also remembered the Civil War and the amount of bloodshed that had been associated with removing a king. It was true that James was only a prospective king but any attempts to remove him from the succession would surely stir the same passions and produce similarly unpleasant results. The issues were finely balanced and, in the absence of further developments, Parliament might have been tempted to back off. In fact, there was about to be a very serious development. Parliament was shortly to be engulfed in turmoil over the Treaty of Dover and, shortly thereafter, England herself was to be engulfed in turmoil over rumours of the Popish Plot.

Even after he had abandoned the war against the Dutch, Charles had sought money from Louis. Louis cannot have reacted happily to this request but when he heard that, bowing to popular pressure, Charles and his brother had agreed that James' daughter, Mary, should marry William of Orange, Louis' patience was exhausted.

Louis no longer saw Charles as a helpful ally. Indeed, the marriage between Mary and William would very likely bring England back into the war on the Dutch side. Louis' best hope was not to support Charles but rather to sow dissension in his realm. So Louis revealed to the Parliamentary opposition in Westminster that Charles' ministers had sought money from the French court. Parliament was furious. Doubtless many already knew of the secret treaty and even more had guessed, but the confirmation was still a blow to Charles. Consider the prestige that was supposed to attach not just to the institution of the monarchy but to the person of the monarch. The concept of Divine Right had not been wholly forgotten; many Englishmen had loyally fought for Charles' rights and under Charles' command. Now they heard that the object of their loyalty cared nothing for their interests and had betrayed them for foreign gold. And they had to hear this from the French.

Sadly the ensuing debates preceded Hansard so we have no proper record of what was said, but we can imagine the indignation, the drama and the palpable sense of betrayal. This would greatly strengthen the Parliamentary hand. Once again Charles' opponents seemed to be riding the wave of history. Fate was about to deliver them a further boost: in the form of the Reverend Titus Oates.

Crackpot conspiracy theorists are not the invention of the Internet age. They have thrived for centuries and one of their most famous representatives lived in seventeenth-century London.

Oates was not a man whose views deserved any credence. Even the most enthusiastic recruitment consultant would have struggled to find the positives in his CV. He had been kicked out of two Cambridge colleges, been imprisoned for perjury and been discharged from the Royal Navy. He had then become a Roman Catholic and been dismissed from a number of Jesuit organisations. Alas, this uninspiring background did not stop people taking him seriously when he announced that there was a Roman Catholic plot to kill the King and establish a Roman Catholic on the throne. In what may have been a rare instance of keen judgment on his part (but which might just as possibly have been a stroke of luck), he named Edward Coleman, private secretary to the Duchess of York, as the lynchpin of the plot. When Coleman's house was searched and his papers examined, they were found to contain a number of documents in which he wrote in favour of the re-establishment of the Roman Catholic Church in England and in which he complained that Charles had not gone further to promote the interests of his Roman Catholic subjects. It was not surprising that a Roman Catholic would have held such views and, even if it was imprudent to commit them to paper, they hardly amounted to evidence of a plot to kill Charles. Any reasonable assessment would have cleared Coleman of any guilt. But these were not reasonable times, especially where religion was concerned.

Many believed that Oates was onto something and that Coleman's correspondence proved the case. Their belief was strengthened when the magistrate trying the case was found stabbed to death. The mob needed no convincing that the Catholics had killed the judge to stop him pronouncing Coleman guilty and as a warning to those who might replace him on the Bench.

Fears of the Popish Plot had reached fever pitch. Those who wanted to bar a Catholic from the throne could hardly have hoped for more auspicious circumstances. Some Parliamentarians decided that it was time to take the plunge.

Of all the steps that Parliament had taken thus far, this was easily the most significant. They had made great in-roads into royal power but, unlike in 1649, they had stopped short of challenging the Stuarts' right to rule. They now wanted to prevent Charles' heir, the Duke of York, from taking the crown.

Charles had been forced to accept the growth of Parliamentary power and the corresponding diminution of his own authority, but the Exclusion Crisis stirred deeper passions. The lawful descent of the Crown was a subject on which he would not budge. The stage was set for confrontation but Charles had one major advantage: his opponents agreed that they did not want James, but they were divided over the question of who should replace him.

Those at the more moderate end of the spectrum wanted the succession to follow its established route but to skip a generation and go to James' daughter Mary (a Protestant). Unless James and his new wife were to have a son, Mary would come to the throne anyway so this would simply accelerate proceedings. Even if there would be some doubts about the validity of Mary's reign during her father's lifetime, on James' death, Mary's claim would be incontestable. Not only that, but Mary was married to the Protestant hero William of Orange. William had enjoyed great success in his wars against the Catholic France and he ruled Holland in a semi-constitutional fashion. For the English Crown to be associated with so fine a ruler seemed an advantage to many.

Others, however, thought that there would be insuperable tensions if Mary were promoted over her father. Even if he wished to avoid it, James could hardly help operating a rival court and, as everyone knew that James would not wish to avoid it, there was the question of whether Mary would be able to take sufficiently decisive action to curb her father's ambitions. If you doubted that Mary would have the strength for this, then was it not also reasonable to fear that she might fall under paternal influence? If this happened then James would become the de facto ruler and the "Exclusion" would be meaningless. Equally, not everyone was keen to see William come to England. They remembered the failure of the Dutch war and disliked the idea that the former enemy leader could establish himself in London's royal palaces.

Those who did not wish to see Mary ascend the throne had an alternative candidate readily available in James, Duke of Monmouth. Monmouth was the King's beloved but illegitimate eldest son. He had been given a clutch of public offices and had commanded some of our troops in the Third Anglo-Dutch War. Given that his name had been mentioned in connection with a murder and a mutilation he was not necessarily an ideal candidate for civilised kingship, but, for some, the fact that he was a Protestant and Charles' son put him well ahead of the Duke of York. Some of Monmouth's supporters wanted the King to legitimise his eldest son. Others thought that there was no need for this; they believed that he was already legitimate.

Monmouth was born during Charles' pre-Restoration exile. His mother was Lucy Walters and there were rumours (supported, unsurprisingly, by Monmouth himself) that she and Charles were married. If so, Monmouth would be legitimate and the lawful heir apparent. The problem would be proving this to be true. It was said that there was evidence of the marriage and that it was contained in a mysterious "black box". If it existed, however, the evidence did not come to light and, as Charles maintained that he had only ever been married to Queen Catherine, Monmouth remained a bastard.

This division between Mary's supporters and those who favoured Monmouth proved a blessing to Charles. Parliaments kept proposing the Exclusion Bill and the King kept dismissing Parliaments but, as long as his adversaries were divided amongst themselves, Charles could get away with delaying the moment of truth. When the time finally came and (at a Parliament convened in safely Royalist Oxford) the King confronted his opponents, the fervour of the Popish Plot had cooled and the divisions in the Exclusionists had become apparent. This meant both that there was less rabidly anti-Catholic support for the principle of Exclusion and that people realised the drawbacks of the practice of Exclusion. Once people could see that pressing the point of Exclusion would be likely to lead to civil war between Monmouth and the supporters of Mary, enthusiasm rapidly fell away. Charles had lost much to Parliament but on the final point, which was also the one about which he cared the most, he had come out on top. James retained his place in the succession and, in due course, would accede to the throne as the legitimate Stuart heir. Perhaps Charles suspected that his brother's reign would be both unhappy and short but he could not be held responsible for that; he would pass the sacred birthright to the next in line and, in doing so, fulfil the most important duty that a monarch owes to his dynasty.

That says it all about Charles II in particular and the Stuarts in general: their loyalty to their dynasty, and to the power that they felt should rightfully attach to that dynasty, trumped all other considerations. The idea of a monarch serving his or her people and working for the best interests of the nation at whose head they had been placed simply did not occur to them. As long as the Stuarts could rule absolutely in England they did not mind how many Englishmen died in civil wars and they did not care if they had to accept bribes from foreign rulers.

Like the Golden Bull and the Spanish Match, the Secret Treaty of Dover shows us how fragile English sovereignty has been. Just as King John and Mary I had feared for their thrones and looked for support elsewhere, so Charles took French gold to shore up his position at home. In doing so he abandoned England's sovereignty and turned himself into a puppet king. So desperate was Charles to avoid sharing power at home that he would send a good deal of it abroad. Louis called the tune and took us into a war that was against English interests. However, just as John and Mary had found, the English will not long be tricked out of their independence. When Charles' position weakened, Parliament lost no time in pouncing. Charles may have won over the Exclusion Crisis but, in every other respect, he was humbled by the House of Commons. In the long term, English liberty emerged not just intact but strengthened.

Postscript – The Stuarts and Monmouth's black box

By way of a postscript it is only fair to note that, while they made lousy kings, the Stuarts' progeny have made excellent subjects. Charles II's bastard sons were advanced to the highest rank of the aristocracy and many of their descendants have served their country and its monarchy with great skill and steadfastness. It may even be that the senior illegitimate Stuart line has gone some way towards atoning for the family sin of valuing dynasty above country.

The Duke of Monmouth's eldest son became the Duke of Buccleuch, and there is an interesting story about the third Duke of Buccleuch. It is said that this Duke discovered the "black box" and found within it the evidence of marriage between Charles II and Lucy Walters. This, of course, meant that Monmouth was legitimate and should by right have succeeded to the throne in place of James II. Barring the intervening legislation governing the succession, it gave the Duke a powerful claim to the Crown. According to the story, the Duke felt such loyalty to the country and was so reluctant to risk any doubt being cast on the title of the reigning sovereign that he destroyed all the evidence[6]. We cannot know if this is true but, if it is, it goes some way to redeeming the Stuart name from the infamy in which it should otherwise be held.

---

[6] The other version of the story is that the Duke showed the evidence to Queen Victoria and that the Queen destroyed it herself.

The Glorious Revolution

A persistent myth about American politics is that, in order to be President, you need both to be a US citizen and to have been born in the United States. The actual phrasing of the relevant requirement is that you need to be a "natural born citizen of the United States". Various US constitutional scholars take the view that the child of two US citizens would be a natural born US citizen even if he or she were born in Cuba, Vietnam or North Korea. Whatever the situation across the pond, English history would have been very different if we had applied an equivalent rule here.

For a start, 30% of the kings and queens since the Norman Conquest would have been ineligible from birth. Henry V could not have led us to victory at Agincourt, Henry VII could not have founded the Tudor dynasty and the King James Bible would be a glory of Scottish literature little known south of the Border. Excluding the foreign-born would also have caused further problems lower down the ranks of the British State. One Prime Minister would have been barred from Downing Street while Canterbury would have had a very different collection of Archbishops.

If the absence of Toulouse-born Bernard Andre from the ranks of our Poets Laureate strikes you as unimportant, consider the dire consequences had Swedish-born Sven-Göran Eriksson been precluded from taking charge of England's football team. We are, and have long been, open to foreign talent. One area that you would think we would keep in-house, though, is revolution.

Most countries run their own revolutions. The Russian Tsar was overthrown by Russian democrats (who were later themselves overthrown by Russian communists). The French did not ask the Danes to oust Louis XVI and the Chinese got rid of their last Emperor without any help from Korea. The English (as is our wont) have done things differently.

History has dubbed the Revolution of 1688 as "Glorious". We remember the triumph of Parliament and the defeat of tyranny. We celebrate the bloodless ousting of the dictatorial James II and the establishment of Protestant liberty. We applaud the foundation of a balanced political settlement in which monarchy and democracy both held places of honour. However, while we recall the Revolution itself, we tend to pay less attention to its leader. This would strike the rest of the world as bizarre. The United States named their capital city after George Washington and, in Russia and China, you can still visit the preserved bodies of Lenin and Mao. What about the hero of 1688? Who was the Glorious Revolutionary and why do we not pay greater respect to him?

The answer is that he was a Dutchman called Willem van Oranje and that, despite all the good he did for England, we have never quite managed to see him as an English hero. He may have done some good work in 1688 but his life before 1688 contains some serious black marks.

Not only was he a foreigner but he had been an active and successful enemy – it had been Willem who had led the Dutch forces to victory over England in the Third Anglo-Dutch War. It takes industrial-scale rebranding to turn so ardent an opponent into a national hero. And in many ways, as we will see, things got worse when Willem became William and moved to London. When King William took charge England suddenly had to march to Holland's tune. There were those who saw the Glorious Revolution as a Dutch Conquest.

As we review the 1688 Revolution we will see that, while it certainly brought much that was good, these benefits were not obtained without sacrifice. The question is whether the sacrifice was worthwhile and whether we gained more than we lost. In considering the events of 1688 we will see the nuances that attend a proper consideration of sovereignty and of sovereignty's relationship to national interest. Our starting point is the accession of James II.

James II's reign began in 1685 on the death of his elder brother, Charles II. It seemed that the impossible had happened: a Roman Catholic had come to the throne of Protestant England. It is worth pausing to remember the extent to which Catholics were feared and hated in seventeenth-century England.

Part of the problem was that they seemed to have an unhealthy obsession with fire. Mary I couldn't see a Protestant without wanting to burn him at the stake, Guy Fawkes was happiest trying to blow up Parliament and it was Papists who started the Great Fire of London (or so every right-thinking Englishman fervently, if rather inaccurately, believed). Belief in transubstantiation seemed to walk hand in hand with extreme pyromania.

The last thing anyone wanted was for Catholics to have any say in the running of the Government and, with that in mind, Catholics had been barred from public offices. Being in communion with the Pope had meant that James had been required to resign his post as Lord High Admiral. His religion would have barred him from any other military appointment just as it would have barred him from the House of Commons, from the judges' bench and from the guild of parish clerks. Roman Catholics were not trusted to serve the English state; it must have seemed bizarre that a Catholic could be trusted to rule as king. Yet here James was: Catholic, proud and King of England. Given the memories of Bloody Mary, the passions that had been inflamed by the rumoured Popish Plot and the ominous example of Catholic tyranny presented by Louis XIV across the Channel in France, one would have thought that James' subjects would have greeted his accession with apprehension and perhaps with armed opposition. In fact, there was widespread rejoicing.

Part of this may be put down to relief at a clear and undisputed succession. The last time that a King had peacefully taken the throne on the death of his predecessor had been when Charles I had succeeded James I in 1625; there were few alive who remembered that. Many more remembered the Civil War, the uncertainty after the death of Cromwell and the divisions exposed during the Exclusion Crisis. The latter point would have been uppermost in people's minds. It had not been a foregone conclusion that the political class would accept James; some elements might have favoured Charles II's illegitimate son, the Duke of Monmouth, while others could have backed James' daughter, Mary. Had that happened, civil war would very likely have returned. In fact, the vast majority had supported James. A Catholic king must have seemed a small price to pay for peace.

The relief will have been compounded by all the promise of a new reign. Honeymoon periods are not just a feature of elected governments. People could look to the future with hope and optimism. After all, though he was a Catholic himself, James had not actually challenged the establishment of the Church of England, nor had he evinced any intention of introducing arbitrary rule. Moreover, he only had two children: Mary and Anne. Both were Protestants. Following the death of their mother, James had married the Catholic Mary of Modena but they were yet to have a child who survived more than a few days. People could expect that James' reign would be but a brief aberration and that, when he died, the more congenial *status quo ante* of Protestant sovereigns would reassert itself.

Even at the time some must have seen that there were a lot of "what ifs" in the hopeful attitude that characterised the early weeks of James' reign. What if James did try to challenge the Church of England? What if he did seek to establish absolute rule? And, crucially, what if he did father a son?

These issues would come to the fore after, and as a direct result of, the first serious challenge to his rule. That challenge would come from his nephew.

The Duke of Monmouth, "our beloved Protestant Duke" as he was known, was Charles II's eldest son. He may have been illegitimate but there were no real doubts as to his parentage. Quite apart from an uncanny resemblance to Charles II, Monmouth was a fast-living, heavy-drinking, bed-hopping young man with all the arrogance bred by decades in the tradition of Divine Right kingship. He was indeed his father's son. Nor was he prepared to let his illegitimacy get in the way of a shining future. Surely, Monmouth reasoned, the English would rather have the Protestant son of Charles II as king in place of James. Monmouth was living in exile on the continent when the fateful change in reign occurred. Though he had few supporters with him, he was confident that his popularity in his native land and the instinctively anti-Catholic views of James' subjects would see the people flock to his banner should he ever land in England and lay claim to the throne. Monmouth was not slow to put these hopes to the test.

In the summer of 1685, Monmouth and his small band arrived in the West Country. He proclaimed his intention to seize his father's throne and to rid England of its Catholic king. "Protestantism and Liberty" was his cry. From small beginnings he soon built a sizeable army. This army had many of the qualities from which battlefield success arises. Its soldiers were loyal to their leader and dedicated to their cause. It was intending to fight on home ground. It was composed very largely of men from the same counties who felt a high degree of comradeship. However, if the rebel army had a number of advantages, there were also many things that it was missing. Military experience for one. The majority of its "soldiers" were agricultural labourers and few had ever seen a battlefield. Equipment was another weak spot. This was not a well-financed operation and Monmouth had been unable to provide much by way of weapons. Plowshares had to be turned into swords and pruninghooks into spears. It should have been obvious that this rebellion would not survive an encounter with an experienced army.

Monmouth's only viable chance of success was to play a long game. If he waited and allowed the size of his army to swell then the balance of opinion in the country might swing in his favour, James might lose his nerve and Monmouth might be able to take the country unopposed. Alas for his supporters, Monmouth was utterly incapable of playing a long game.

When word reached Monmouth's ears that the James and his army were nearing the rebels' position, the Duke decided to meet them in buccaneering style. As soon as the King's army had arrived in the West Country and pitched camp for the night, Monmouth was on the scene. He led his men in a midnight raid. As daring as it was futile, this raid brought the rebellion to an end before it had properly begun. Monmouth's men did their best but the King's army was well trained, well equipped and battle-hardened. Despite the fact that many of the King's soldiers had literally been caught napping, they were still able to make short work of the rebels. After a brief stint on the run, Monmouth was captured and brought to London. He was imprisoned in the Tower and then executed for treason – just as his grandfather had been all those decades before.

Despite his victory, James was left deeply shaken by Monmouth's rebellion. As he sat in Whitehall he considered the position. He wanted to rule as an absolute monarch and he wanted England to be a Roman Catholic country. The recent revolt had shown him how much opposition both elements of this ambition would face. Some monarchs would have learnt their lesson and abandoned their hopes for tyranny. James, however, had inherited the full measure of Stuart obduracy. He would not be dissuaded from his course; indeed, he would accelerate his progress. The English people would have to be crushed into obedience. His army had shown itself to be a formidable fighting force and James had used the rebellion to make the army considerably larger than it had previously been and even more loyal to him personally than it had been before. He had recruited large numbers of new soldiers and he had also, in flagrant breach of the Test Act, appointed a large number of Roman Catholics to positions as army officers.

A Roman Catholic King at the head of a large Roman Catholic-led army chilled the heart of Protestant England. Parliament and the people wanted the Catholic officers to be dismissed and the army to be reduced in size. James had no intention of playing ball. The third Stuart in a row was about to enter into conflict with his people. On 9th November 1685, the King set out his stall[7].

James went to Westminster and addressed both Houses of Parliament. He began by praising God for the victory over Monmouth but soon trespassed into more dangerous territory. He told Parliament not only that he intended to keep all of his Catholic officers but that he intended to maintain and enlarge the army. The King then asked Parliament to vote the necessary supply.

The gauntlet had been thrown down indeed.

The King had shown his true colours. His speech had been nothing short of a manifesto for tyranny, and James had asked Parliament to become his accomplice in carrying it out. Parliament was not just a turkey being asked to vote for Christmas, it was a turkey being asked to pay for and to sharpen the butcher's axe.

MPs and peers knew that the stakes were high. They could defy the King, and invite civil war – or they could agree to his demands, and invite Catholic dictatorship. Neither option was attractive and both would have serious consequences. For the individual Parliamentarians involved, of course, capitulation would have been the safer course. To challenge royal authority was to court the severest punishment. The House of Lords lacked the stomach for

[7]http://www.british-history.ac.uk/report.aspx?compid=40482

such fight; but the House of Commons was made of sterner stuff. After lengthy debate, the Commons voted to confront the King.

The House of Commons sent James a powerful Address[8]. MPs said that Catholic officers held their commissions illegally and that James had no power to override the Test Act or any other law. They told the King that such officers would have to be dismissed and that Parliament would not vote supply for a standing army. Though couched in the phraseology of grovelling subjects (with lots of "humble beseeching" etc) the substance of the document was explosive. If James had thrown down the gauntlet, the Commons had picked it up.

England's politics were on a knife edge. People waited nervously to see what would happen next. It was now clear that they had a King who was intent on despotism and a political class determined to stand for freedom. A straight fight between them would be bloody and the result would be uncertain. Happily this was no more appealing to James than it was to his people. While the King would have been quite happy to fight Parliament if victory had been assured, he was unwilling to risk everything if there was a chance that he might lose. James therefore determined to play for time and see what support he had elsewhere in the Establishment. The army was on his side but Parliament was against him; what about the law courts?

James realised that Parliament was not the only body who could pronounce on the legality of his actions. Judges, as keepers of Common Law, held a place of honour in the English constitution. If they could be prevailed upon to say that the King was above the law and could validly appoint Catholic officers whatever the Test Act said, then this would undercut the politicians. With the backing of

---

[8] http://www.british-history.ac.uk/report.aspx?compid=40482

the army and of the courts, James' position would look secure indeed.

This was top-class creative thinking on James' part. Rather than declaring war on Parliament, he would dissolve it and tell MPs that he would see them in court. James quickly put his plan into action. There were two immediate questions: could a test case be arranged and could the King be sure that he would receive the judicial support he needed? James set out to get the right answers to both of those questions.

The first point was to arrange for the test case. Just like a modern ambulance-chaser, James set out to spur a would-be claimant into the courts. The King needed someone to bring legal proceedings against a Catholic officer alleging that the officer in question held his office in breach of the Test Act. The officer would claim that there had been no breach because the King had "dispensed" with the Test Act. The judges would then have to decide whether such a dispensation was legally effective.

The Catholic officer whom James chose was Sir Edward Hales. Sir Edward was the perfect defendant for the case James needed to see. He was a Catholic but, despite this, James had appointed him to command a regiment of foot guards. At James' order one of Sir Edward's servants, Arthur Godden, informed the magistrates and claimed that Sir Edward was in breach of the Test Act. The case was eventually heard at the Court of King's Bench.

So James had the case he wanted; would he also get the answer he wanted? That was far from certain. The judges may have been members of the King's Bench but they were not royal placemen. They were experienced lawyers and they were steeped in the traditions of English jurisprudence. They knew that the Common Law is a law of freedom, not of repression, and they knew that it offers no place for autocrats. If matters were left to take their course fairly, Sir Edward would be dismissed from his post and the King would receive an indirect judicial rebuke. Letting matters take the course fairly, however, was not James' way. He soon got to work on the judges.

He bullied some, threatened others and bribed some more. Some of the more intransigent judges were prevailed upon to recuse themselves and those who saw some merit in Sir Edward's case were encouraged to exaggerate that merit. The result was that, by a verdict of eleven to one, the Court of King's Bench concluded that the King could indeed dispense with the Test Act. The Lord Chief Justice stated:

> 1) that the kings of England are sovereign princes;
>
> 2) that the laws of England are the king's laws;
>
> 3) that therefore it is an inseparable prerogative in the kings of England to dispense with penal [i.e. anti-Catholic] laws in particular cases and upon particular necessary reasons;
>
> 4) that of those reasons and those necessities, the king himself is sole judge; and then, which is consequent upon all,
>
> 5) that this is not a trust invested in, or granted to, the king by the people, but the ancient remains of the sovereign power and prerogative of the kings of England; which never yet was taken from them, nor can be[9].

Some say that "Justice must not only be done; it must be paid to be done"; well, James' bribes had certainly worked their magic on the judges. Their venal and cowardly judgment set its face against centuries of Parliamentary evolution. It was an interpretation of the law that would have struck many as outdated even in the reign of Elizabeth I. The Lord Chief Justice had announced his opinion that

---

[9] http://www.jacobite.ca/documents/1686godden.htm

the King of England was legally entitled to reign as a tyrant. The courts had come up trumps and given the King a legal victory. He could have his Catholic officers and, according to the courts, he had the power to dispense with laws as he saw fit. Few doubted what the King's next step would be. There was a host of laws with which he wanted to dispense. He wanted to free Roman Catholics from the restrictions of the Penal Laws. Just as he had turned from Parliament to the courts in order to be confirmed in his power to dispense with laws, James would now turn from the courts to another great institution in order to carry out that dispensation. He would ask the Church of England to proclaim Catholic Toleration.

This was not (quite) as crackers an idea as it may now seem. The Church of England was, of course, proudly Protestant and keenly anti-Catholic but it was also devoted to royal power. Its doctrine of Non-Resistance held that it was a sin to defy the King's will. James meant to make the most of this.

The King drafted the Declaration of Indulgence. This dispensed with the Penal Laws and granted religious freedom to all his subjects – even the Roman Catholic ones. James then ordered that the Declaration be read from every pulpit in the land. Surely, he reasoned, the non-resisting clergymen would have no choice but to comply. He thought that the vicars would crumble as had the judges. He was wrong – there proved to be more mettle in the mitre and crosier than in the wig and gavel.

On 13th May the Archbishop of Canterbury met with the Bishops of London, Bristol, Chichester, Ely, Peterborough and St Asaph. They were to decide whether or not the Church would follow the commands of the King or, as they saw it, the will of God. The Almighty is used to coming second to the more immediate demands of worldly pressures but, in this instance, He came out on top. The Bishops would defy the King.

The Seven Bishops wrote to the King petitioning him to think again and saying that they would not allow the Declaration of Indulgence to be read in their dioceses. The Declaration of Indulgence, they said, represented the unilateral repeal of a Parliamentary statute. As well as being contrary to the law of God it ran counter to the law of the land. The Bishops wanted no part in it.

In their attitude to the King, the Bishops had followed Parliament rather than the courts. They would meet the same hostile response from James. While, unlike Parliament, the Bishops could not be dissolved on a royal whim, they could be prosecuted for their disobedience. James had every reason to believe that the judges would do his bidding so he determined to rely on the courts again and to put the Bishops on trial. This turned out to be a PR disaster.

The Bishops were sent to the Tower pending trial, but the Canterbury Seven (as the modern tabloids would surely have named them) won an early victory in the court of public opinion. The people rushed onto the streets to protest against the King and in favour of the Bishops. The Bishop of Bristol, Jonathan Trelawny, was descended from an old Cornish family and became a particular hero in his native county. While, sadly, it was penned many years after the event, *The Song of the Western Men* captures something of the spirit that pervaded the Bishops' trial:

> "*A good sword and a trusty hand!*
> *A faithful heart and true!*
> *King James's men shall understand*
> *What Cornish lads can do!*
> *And have they fixed the where and when?*
> *And shall Trelawny die?*
> *Here's twenty thousand Cornish men*
> *Will know the reason why!*"

Whether the judges bowed to popular pressure or felt moved to by the shame of their feeble decision in the Sir Edward Hales case we will never know. Whatever the reason, the court gave judgment in favour of the Bishops. The King had lost. More than that, he had been caught trying to assert absolute power in favour of the Catholics by trampling on the interests of the Protestants' leaders. He had confirmed his subjects' worst suspicions and he had done so at the worst possible time because the stakes were about to get much higher: James was about to have a son.

The birth of James' son (also called James and known to history as the Old Pretender) was not accompanied by the rejoicing that would usually follow the arrival of an heir to the throne. The people knew that the heir would be raised a Catholic. Suddenly, a Catholic king began to look less like a weird departure from normality and more like the status quo in waiting. A brief Catholic interlude of one reign's duration might be bearable; a long line of Catholic kings was not.

Indeed, so eager were the people to dodge this hateful prospect, they decided that the Queen had not really given birth at all. Rather they believed the rumour that a changeling had been smuggled into the Queen's bedroom in a warming pan and had dishonestly been adopted as a royal prince[10]. History has doubted that the Warming Pan Plot really took place and has assumed that the baby was James and Mary's legitimate son. Whatever the rights and wrongs of that, the baby, and the future that he embodied, were desperately unpopular. For a small but powerful group of English statesmen, a Catholic heir was the last straw and they determined to act.

The number seven seems to have been important at this stage of England's history and, just as seven Bishops defied James over the

---

[10]The danger that this might recur meant that, in future, the Home Secretary would attend royal births to watch for any foul play (this custom continued until the birth of the late Princess Margaret).

Declaration of Indulgence, now seven politicians (strictly six politicians and one bishop) would defy the King's right to reign.

The Immortal Seven, as they have become known, were: the Earls of Danby, Devonshire and Shrewsbury, the Viscount Lumley, Edward Russell, Henry Sydney and the Bishop of London. They could no longer stomach James as King and determined to replace him. They soon realised that the answer lay in Holland.

Discounting James' young son, his daughter Mary was heir to the throne. Mary was married to the Dutch leader, William of Orange. William was a bold leader and gifted military tactician and, just as the English today go to Holland in search of pharmaceutical freedom, so, in the seventeenth century, the Immortal Seven would look to Holland for Protestant freedom. It was to William that the Immortal Seven wrote:

> "The people are so generally dissatisfied with the present conduct of the government in relation to their religion, liberties and properties (all which have been greatly invaded), and they are in such expectation of their prospects being daily worse, that your Highness may be assured there are nineteen parts of twenty of the people throughout the kingdom who are desirous of a change, and who, we believe, would willingly contribute to it.[11]"

The main substance of the Invitation was the following conditional promise:

> "if the circumstances stand so with your Highness that you believe you can get here time enough, in a condition to give assistances this year sufficient for a relief under these circumstances which have been now represented, we who subscribe this will not fail to attend your Highness upon your

[11] http://faculty.history.wisc.edu/sommerville/351/WIIIinvite.html

> landing and to do all that lies in our power to prepare others to be in as much readiness as such an action is capable of'.

The Immortal Seven took a tremendous risk. Had this letter fallen into James' hands he would have denounced it as treason and thrown all the resources of the State into punishing the perpetrators. They were risking their lives to rid their country of a dictatorial king. How, though, would William respond?

Perhaps we should first ask how William *should* have responded. He was being asked to undertake to invade and conquer a foreign country. He would have to find and fund an army; he would have to ask his troops to risk their lives in the effort; and he would have to face the consequences if it all went pear-shaped. True, Holland had done well in some of her previous wars with England, but those conflicts had been fought on the high seas. Things might well be different if he tried to battle the English on land and, indeed, on their home turf. Clearly, if things went well there would be a fair amount of glory in liberating Protestant England from the prospect of Catholic despotism, but the main winners from his victory would be the English. Why, frankly, should William lift a finger to help them? The answer was that by helping them he might very well be able to help himself.

England was a wealthy and powerful country. Her resources could be a deciding factor in Holland's war with Catholic France. If William could make himself master of these resources, he could also use them to make himself Holland's saviour.

The Immortal Seven saw that England was in jeopardy and they wanted William to liberate her. William saw that England was up for grabs and planned to seize control of her. There was a vast gulf between the aims of the Immortal Seven and the hopes of their would-be saviour. For the instant, however, this gulf was unclear.

When William accepted their invitation the Immortal Seven rejoiced. The Glorious Revolution was underway.

At first it seemed that Providence had declared against the Revolution; the wind was not favourable for a Channel crossing and William's fleet was blown back into port. Fate, however, was simply storing up a public relations coup for William and his men. When, finally, "the Protestant wind" began to blow they set sail and the delay meant that William landed in Torbay on 5th November. 5th November already held a treasured place in England's folk memory. Minds turned to another occasion when Papists had sought to undermine English freedom by challenging (or rather, in the case of Mr Fawkes and his crew, blowing up) Parliament. Could there have been a more auspicious day for a Protestant champion to land in England? More importantly, would William be able to make the most of this happy chronological coincidence?

Certainly he was, militarily speaking, in a far stronger position than Monmouth had been when he had tried to usurp the throne. Against the urgings of his English supporters, William had come to England at the head of a large Dutch and mercenary army. The Immortal Seven wanted William to rely on English support and to avoid using foreign troops to fight the English army and shed English blood. What William saw (and what the Immortal Seven missed) was that this English support would come in rather more quickly if William could show that he was serious. A rerun of Monmouth's failed expedition would attract little backing. The surest way to rally support in England (and thus avoid pitched battle) was to make it clear that, if a pitched battle could not be avoided, William would win it. People felt more comfortable in pledging their allegiance to the commander of a large army of battle-hardened troops.

William was right, but it was the first sign of the compromises that the Immortal Seven would have to accept. The Immortal Seven hoped that William's leadership would benefit the rebels' cause;

they did not want to welcome a Dutch invasion force. That, however, is exactly what they were forced to do. Before it had even started, the sheen was starting to come off the Glorious Revolution.

Having landed in England and sitting at the head of his troops, William decided to wait. He did not intend to push James into war. Rather he would allow time for his support to swell, for James' to collapse and for the balance of power to tilt in his direction. Initial signs were favourable. Senior nobles declared for William and the people joined anti-Catholic riots and uprisings. Despite this, it seemed that James would not give in without a fight. By late November the English army had come to meet the Dutch invaders near Salisbury and James himself had joined his forces. Battle looked likely. James, however, had pushed his people too far. Many of James' officers and soldiers were fed up with fighting for a Catholic and against Protestants and there were mass desertions to William's side. The future Duke of Marlborough (ancestor of Winston Churchill) abandoned the King only hours after an enthusiastic declaration of loyalty. Back in London, Princess Anne (James' daughter and William's sister-in-law) also quit James' cause. James could see the writing on the wall. There was no point leading his reduced army into a losing battle. It was time to retreat.

James dashed back to the capital to collect some belongings before trying to flee England on 11th December[12]. His disguise was rumbled and he was sent back to London. William held the life of his uncle and father-in-law in his hands. Had the situation been reversed and had William been James' prisoner it is likely that he would have met the same fate as Monmouth. The execution of a close relative would, however, have made a poor start to his reign so William agreed to turn a blind eye and allow James to slip away to

[12] This seems to be a good day for royal exile –it was on 11th December 1936 that the Duke of Windsor sailed into exile after the Abdication

France. James left a novel problem behind him: England was without a king.

How to proceed? Ideally Parliament should have been called but it was far from clear that this could be done. After all, the English Parliament could only be called by an English monarch. No such person was readily available. Importantly, neither William nor Mary was yet judged to have the requisite royal power. The lawyers scratched their heads. In the circumstances the best that could be managed was to summon a Convention Parliament. Once assembled, it was this Convention Parliament that offered the Crown to William and Mary.

This in itself is one of the reasons that the Revolution was indeed glorious. William's claim to the throne was not based on royal blood or on conquest; it was based on Parliamentary decree. This was a clear sign of the new power that Parliament was accruing.

Next came the Bill of Rights. It was in the Bill of Rights that Parliament, "vindicating and asserting their ancient rights and liberties", declared:

> That the pretended power of suspending the laws or the execution of laws by regal authority without consent of Parliament is illegal;
>
> That the pretended power of dispensing with laws or the execution of laws by regal authority, as it hath been assumed and exercised of late, is illegal;
>
> That levying money for or to the use of the Crown by pretence of prerogative, without grant of Parliament, for longer time, or in other manner than the same is or shall be granted, is illegal;

That the raising or keeping a standing army within the kingdom in time of peace, unless it be with consent of Parliament, is against law;

That the subjects which are Protestants may have arms for their defence suitable to their conditions and as allowed by law;

That election of members of Parliament ought to be free;

That the freedom of speech and debates or proceedings in Parliament ought not to be impeached or questioned in any court or place out of Parliament;

That excessive bail ought not to be required, nor excessive fines imposed, nor cruel and unusual punishments inflicted;

That jurors ought to be duly impanelled and returned, and jurors which pass upon men in trials for high treason ought to be freeholders;

That all grants and promises of fines and forfeitures of particular persons before conviction are illegal and void;

And that for redress of all grievances, and for the amending, strengthening and preserving of the laws, Parliaments ought to be held frequently.

And they do claim, demand and insist upon all and singular the premises as their undoubted rights and liberties, and that no declarations, judgments, doings or proceedings to the prejudice of the people in any of the said premises ought in any wise to be drawn hereafter into consequence or example"[13].

---

[13]http://www.historylearningsite.co.uk/bill_of_rights.htm

All this speaks of a Glorious Revolution. A tyrannical monarch had been deposed and Parliament had made it clear that it would decide who ruled England. Parliament had moreover taken the opportunity to state a host of liberties that would henceforward be sacrosanct. These are remarkable achievements on their own terms, but when we consider how close James had brought us to absolutism and how little armed strife had been engendered to bring this change about, one can certainly see why the adjective Glorious seems appropriate.

There is, however, rather more to this story than meets the eye. Firstly, many in Parliament actively did not want William to be King. The Tories in the House of Commons and the majority of the House of Lords were loyal to the legitimate succession. The purists amongst them did not believe in the concept of abdication; as long as James had breath in his body, he would be the rightful King of England. The more moderate traditionalists wanted Mary (James' heir if one ignored his son) to succeed. Neither the purists nor the moderate traditionalists could see how William could be King and the initial proposal to make William co-monarch with Mary was defeated in Parliament. The plan's opponents only changed their minds when William threatened to up sticks and leave unless he were crowned King. Tories and peers are rightly attached to their principles but the English Parliamentarian is first and foremost a pragmatic creature. Faced with the disappearance of the Dutch army and the return of a vengeful James II, they realised that they could after all find room in their lives for William III. Parliament's power and freedom has been somewhat exaggerated. Parliament may have voted to offer the crown to William, but doing so required many Parliamentarians to vote against their consciences and bow to political reality.

As if that were not enough, the political class had to cope with some high-profile Dutch recruits. The Earls of Portland and Albemarle sound like typical huntin', shootin' and fishin' English lords but if you scratch the surface you will find that they were Dutchmen called Hans William Bentinck and Arnold Joost van Keppel. This, to say the least, raised some hackles in Westminster.

Nor were Bentick and van Keppel the only unpopular Dutchmen in London. Even before the Convention Parliament had been called, William had ordered all English troops to leave London and their barracks had been filled by Dutch soldiers (at England's expense). No English soldier would march in London until 1690. A country is enjoying an odd species of freedom when its capital is in the hands of foreign troops and its own regiments are nowhere to be seen.

King William also received a cool welcome elsewhere in the country. It was true that James II had sorely tried the Church of England and it was also true that its vicars had been prepared to defy him on occasion, but many Anglican clergy agreed with the Tories that kingship was a sacred trust and that Parliament had no power to strip the King of his crown. Many priests refused to break the oaths they had sworn to James and, accordingly, they refused to pledge their loyalty to William (becoming known as "non-jurors" for refusing the oath). Five of the Seven Bishops who had opposed James over the Declaration of Indulgence themselves became non-jurors. These five Bishops were ardent Protestants who had resisted the tyranny of James II but they did not regard the events of 1688 as a Glorious Revolution; they saw it as bare-faced treason[14].

Of course, loyalty to James and opposition to William was felt far beyond the parsonages of England. James had also been King of

---

[14] Bizarrely, a small number of non-juror clergymen remained loyal to the Stuarts until 1788 and the death of Bonnie Prince Charlie. At this point the non-jurors received a cruel payback for their fidelity. They had forfeited ecclesiastical preferment, they had subordinated their Protestant instincts and they had accepted that many of their countrymen regarded them as traitors. On Bonnie Prince Charlie's death his brother, Henry, inherited the Stuart claim to the throne and the non-jurors were faced with the ludicrous situation of hailing a Roman Catholic Cardinal as Henry IX.

Scotland and King of Ireland. As a Stuart, James had a particular hold on the hearts of the Scots and as a Catholic he was favoured by many in Ireland. In both countries William and Mary's succession would lead to uprisings and in both countries these uprisings would only be suppressed with much bloodshed. In Ireland the legacy of those years is with us today (the Orangemen, for instance, take their name from William III's family – the House of Orange).

All of this was just within the British Isles; what about foreign affairs? Being King of England was not to be scoffed at but William's main aim was to bring English might to bear against France in support of Holland. The Convention Parliament turned him down but, in September 1689, its successor gave way and consented to William committing England to war against the French. Possibly we would happily have gone to war against the French anyway (we had done so before 1689 and we would do so afterwards) but the fact remains that we had lost freedom of action in the matter. A foreign monarch wanted to look after the land of his birth and he sent English soldiers to fight and die in that cause. This again feels like a funny kind of freedom. Not only were our men sent to war by a foreign king, they were led by foreign officers. During the war, MPs would complain bitterly about English regiments being commanded by Dutch officers, but little progress was made.

So did the events of 1688 amount to a Glorious Revolution or a Dutch Conquest? The answer is that there were elements of both but that, on balance, they amounted more to a Glorious Revolution. This dichotomy is, in itself, an important point. On one level there can be no ambiguity about freedom and sovereignty; but on another level the nature of international politics tends to mean that these concepts are rife with uncertainty. Dispensing with a tyrannical monarch and passing the Bill of Rights were great things; being forced into war and watching foreign troops control London were rather less so. It is possible to advance the national interest by sacrificing sovereignty but this is a heavy step to take and one should be prepared for the consequences. One should, moreover, act swiftly to mitigate those consequences. Perhaps we were too slow to do this with the House of Orange; we were quicker off the mark when it came to the House of Hanover – as we will see in the next chapter.

The Hanoverian Succession

One December during the late 1940s, a current affairs programme on a Washington DC radio station had an interesting idea for their Christmas edition. They telephoned various foreign ambassadors to the United States, asked them what they would like for Christmas and recorded the answers. These were then broadcast on Christmas Day. The French ambassador went for "peace throughout the world" while the Soviet ambassador said that he wanted "freedom for all those enslaved by capitalist imperialism". Britain's ambassador, Sir Oliver Franks, took a different approach. "Well, it's very kind of you to ask," he said, "I'd quite like a box of crystallised fruit."

This (possibly apocryphal) story is sometimes used as an example of a media gaffe and the general view has been that our man in Washington got caught out. I'm not so sure. Sir Oliver, after all, had the last laugh: he was the only ambassador to get what he had asked for.

Sometimes a modest but achievable aim is better than reaching for the stars. It is this sort of thinking that we must keep in mind as we consider the Hanoverian Succession (whereby Georg of Hanover was plucked from German obscurity and placed on the English throne despite the presence of a host of Stuarts who, in traditional theory, were higher up the royal pecking order). The traditional assessment of the Hanoverian Succession is that it was an unmitigated triumph in that it gave us a disinterested foreign king who allowed royal power to fade and gave space for Parliament to take centre stage. Sadly, closer inspection proves that this "triumph" is rather less than it seems. The pros still outweigh the cons but it is, in some respects, closer to a box of crystallised fruit than to worldwide peace.

As we sift the good from the bad we will find ourselves judging everything from the standpoint of overall national interest. Such a standpoint enables us to permit quite serious losses in one area if they will secure even greater benefits elsewhere and if the final position leaves Great Britain on top. So what were the relevant pros and cons?

The positive points have been much praised by historians. Two in particular stand out. The first is that the Hanoverian Succession demonstrated and enhanced the power of Parliament. It was Parliament, rather than straightforward heredity or military conquest, which chose Britain's monarch. Parliament passed an Act that diverted the Crown over dozens of princely heads before depositing it on a German, George I, who had never even visited Britain. It is generally thought that this put Parliament firmly in the driving seat. This does indeed make the Hanoverian Succession look both positive and impressive. And there is more to come.

The second positive point says that choosing a foreigner was a masterstroke. Neither George I nor George II was particularly interested in Britain. This lack of interest created a power vacuum at the head of the British State. That vacuum would be filled by Parliament, by the Cabinet and, most particularly, by the Prime Minister. Elected and accountable figures would henceforth dominate British statecraft. Native-born monarchs, it may be assumed, would have guarded their powers more jealously; a foreign succession meant a less careful succession and this provided opportunities that the political class was well able to exploit. On this reckoning, the Hanoverian Succession accelerated British political development by decades, perhaps, judging from the rest of Europe, by centuries.

All of this good and all of it is true – but it is not the whole story.

George I and George II did indeed care more for Hanover than for Britain, but one consequence of this was that they wanted to use the resources of the latter to advance the interests of the former. There were occasions when our concerns were sacrificed to those of Hanover. Some of our greatest statesmen thought that those instances were a price worth paying for the broader advantages of the Hanoverian Succession; others disagreed.

Furthermore, if Britain sometimes seemed to be subordinated to a foreign power, there were also problems at home. Just as many had struggled fully to acknowledge William III as their king, so there were plenty who could not regard George I as their lawful sovereign. The Hanoverian Succession would see internal dissent and rebellion.

Scratching the surface we therefore see plenty of cons alongside the pros. Before we start to weigh them against each other, however, we must review the background to the Hanoverian Succession. We must see just how dramatic a step it was and we must understand why it came about. To grasp the magnitude of what was proposed, it might be helpful to think of it in modern terms.

The Hanoverian Succession meant diverting the Crown from the first in line (by established rules) to the fifty-sixth in line. At the time of writing the fifty-sixth in line to the throne is the Hon James Lascelles. Mr Lascelles is the youngest son of the late Earl of Harewood, who, in turn, was the son of Princess Mary, the daughter of George V. If we applied the logic of the Hanoverian Succession today, Mr Lascelles would take his place as heir to the throne. I should say that I have never met Mr Lascelles and know of no reason why he would not be a very fine king (indeed he is an accomplished musician who has played at Glastonbury so he might easily find a role championing Britain's creative industries) but this would clearly be a seismic change to the future of the monarchy. Only a particularly alarming state of affairs could justify such radical action. Such a state of affairs certainly existed at the beginning of the eighteenth century.

England had gone to the effort of the Glorious Revolution in order to secure the Protestant succession and keep the main line of the Stuarts off the throne. The hope had been that William and Mary would have children and establish a noble Protestant dynasty, but their marriage proved childless. On William's death, Anne, Mary's sister, took the throne. Again, hopes were high that the Protestant succession would be secured. For eleven years these hopes centred on Anne's son Prince William, Duke of Gloucester. However, Gloucester's short life was marred by illness and he died in 1700. Anne had been pregnant many times but Gloucester was the only one of her children to live beyond their third birthday. Worried minds now turned to the question of the succession. Who would have the best claim to the throne on Anne's death?

The alarming answer was: James Stuart, the Old Pretender. James was the son of the deposed (and now deceased) James II. If the usual rules of royal descent were followed then he should have been king in place of William, Mary and Anne. As such he would surely have the best legal claim on Anne's death. He was, however, an unappealing prospect. He had lived much of his life in France where he had imbibed the full measure of his father's bitterness, of Catholic ritualism and of French absolutism. No one doubted what the reign of James III would mean. King James would seek revenge on those who had overthrown his father, he would impose Catholicism on his Protestant subjects and he would abolish Parliament so that he could rule as a true Stuart tyrant. James III was not a popular king-in-waiting. England had to prevent James coming to the throne in the first place. It was time for a pre-emptive revolution.

Revolutions (even forward-looking ones) need champions. If we were to pull up the drawbridge when faced with James III, we would need to open the door to someone else. The hunt was soon on for a new heir.

In the past, responsibility for England's freedom had lain with soldiers and sailors, with politicians and statesmen and with bishops and judges; now, however, a new band of freedom fighters was called for. Our trust was placed in the hands of a crack troop of elite genealogists. These family history buffs were ordered to the archives on a royal quest: we needed a new monarch – and he or she would have to be Protestant.

Our bold lineage-tracers had their work cut out for them. The branches of the royal family tree spread across Europe. They snaked their way through France, Spain and Savoy. They took in Bohemia, Simmern and Degenfeld. Each family line was diligently pursued. All the royal hatches, matches and dispatches were confirmed. Some branches came to, literally, dead ends. Others were flourishing but were doing so in the Catholic faith and had to be disregarded. Then, just as they were beginning to give up hope, one particularly thorough researcher hit the jackpot: he found Sophia of Hanover.

Sophia's mother, Elizabeth Stuart, was a daughter of James I. Sophia was a Protestant and she had married a Protestant, Ernst Augustus of Brunswick-Lüneburg. Ernst Augustus was not the most important of Germanic princes but he played his hand well and had become Elector of Hanover. Ernst and Sophia also had a number of Protestant children, including a son called Georg. Things were finally looking up. We could have a Protestant Queen with a Protestant heir. On the other hand, the effort that had been required to track her down did not augur well. If it was accepted that she had royal blood in her veins, it had also to be accepted that this royal blood was seriously diluted. Georg's was even more so. Could we really promote the fifty-sixth in line to first place? And if their royal blood was diluted, so was their English blood. Did we really want to import a clutch of second-rate German princelings?

After all, Georg was the future Elector of Hanover and would have loyalties to, and responsibilities for, his German realm. Some predicted that a union of the crowns would end up with Hanover calling the tune in London. It would at the very least be tempting for Georg to use England's considerable resources to advance Hanover's interests. There were concerns, too, about the type of sovereign that Georg would wish to be. Hanover was an absolute monarchy. It was possible that Georg would merely see England as a broader stage on which to practise his tyranny.

Neither of these were minor issues but, ultimately, the potential drawbacks of George I were just that – potential and, therefore, uncertain. The drawbacks of a Catholic restoration (ie a vengeful and absolutist James III) were all too definite. It may have been a risk but the Hanoverian Succession was a risk worth taking.

Parliament therefore passed the Act of Settlement so that, if Queen Anne left no children, Sophia would be next in line to the throne. The Act of Settlement also provided that, thereafter, the throne would go to "the heirs of her body being Protestants". So much for the Catholic Stuarts. Parliament, however, had not forgotten its concerns about these Hanoverians and was eager to make sure that they were not given unfettered power.

Just as Bishop Gardiner had puzzled over the details of the Spanish Match[15], so now the politicians and lawyers set themselves to avoiding a Hanoverian takeover. Their focus was on the Act of Settlement and they were careful in their drafting. Section 3 provided that "in case the crown and imperial dignity of this realm shall hereafter come to any person not being a native of this kingdom of England, this nation be not obliged to engage in any war for the defence of any dominions or territories which do not belong to the crown of England without the consent of Parliament". Good

[15] As we saw in Chapter 2.

thinking but, alas, as Gardiner had found and as we shall see again shortly, law is not the same as politics.

As it happened, Sophia pre-deceased Queen Anne and, on Anne's death in 1714, Georg came to the throne. The spin doctors must have been delighted that the anglicised form of his name was that of England's patron saint. Otherwise, however, his strength lay in what he was not: Stuart, Catholic or intent on despotism.

George provoked little enthusiasm. His arrival in Greenwich on 29 September 1714 was entirely lacking in glamour and romance. The new king was small, plain and drably dressed. His courtiers, too, were an uninspiring lot. None of them could speak English properly and few had any idea of how the British behaved. Even in his choice of mistresses, George managed to disappoint. Charles II had surrounded himself with the great beauties of the age and his people had a sneaking pride in the conquests of their amorous monarch. The charms of George I's mistresses were rather less readily apparent. Unkindness about the physical attributes of those in the public eye is not a twenty-first century phenomenon. George's mistresses received the full measure of public bile. One of George's supposed mistresses was tall and thin and the other was short and fat, and they were nicknamed the Maypole and the Elephant accordingly[16]. None of this advanced George's street cred. George never won the hearts of the British. At the beginning of his reign his coronation was met with surly protest and, at the end, his death engendered little mourning. Actually, things were to get even worse after his death. George was buried in Hanover at Leineschloss and his body (and the rest of the castle) were blown to smithereens by an RAF raid during the Second World War. No, George and the British never did get on.

---

[16] As it happens the "Elephant" was in fact Sophia Charlotte von Kielmansegg, George's half-sister.

To be fair to George it was not all his fault. Part of the problem was that Parliament had given the King a rather diminished form of monarchy. When you start monkeying around with the line of succession you inevitably tarnish some of the magic of kingship. Take, for instance, the practice of touching for the King's Evil. It had long been believed that "the King's Evil" (scrofula to you and me) could be cured by the royal touch. Queen Anne had certainly tried to alleviate her subjects' suffering in this way (Samuel Johnson of Dictionary fame had been one of her patients). People could just about believe that this magical power might be passed down the kingly line but it seemed rather a stretch to think that it would follow Parliamentary direction if, as happened in the case of the Hanoverian Succession, Parliament took it upon itself to choose a new king. George's scrofulous subjects had no interest in trying out the royal touch and the King had to abandon the practice.

This was a small example but a telling one. A much more serious sign of his questionable royalty presented itself early in George's reign and it would dog his successors for years. There were those who were determined to put a Stuart on the throne. They were called Jacobites and they threatened civil war.

As we have seen, James II had died in exile and his son, James Stuart the Old Pretender, had now grown to manhood. The Old Pretender had assumed the headship of the House of Stuart and the leadership of the Stuart cause. His supporters hailed him as James III and VIII and they longed to make this title a political reality. They would invade Britain for him in 1715 and they would invade Britain for his son, the Young Pretender (or Bonnie Prince Charlie) in 1745. The Fifteen was put down with relative ease; the Forty Five was different.

The Bonnie Prince landed in the Highlands and made short work of Government forces at the Battle of Prestonpans before taking Edinburgh. Early victory put a spring into the Jacobite step and they crossed the border into England. They took Carlisle and Preston and got as far south as Derby before losing their nerve. Charles heard that a large part of the British Army had been recalled from action on the Continent. This was too much for him and he swiftly retreated to Scotland. The Young Pretender would make his last stand at the Battle of Culloden. The Jacobite Army was smashed. Thousands of Jacobites died and reprisals against those who survived were brutal. Relations between England and Scotland (relatively recently united in the Kingdom of Great Britain) were soured for years.

Any assessment of the impact of the Hanoverian Succession must give due weight to blood spilt and lives lost in the Jacobite Wars. It must also consider the uncertainty and bitterness that these risings provoked. The conclusion may still be that the Succession was a good bargain but one cannot properly reach a conclusion at all without remembering the Jacobites.

Nor were the Jacobites the only problem to which the Hanoverian Succession gave rise. The Hanoverians were also responsible for introducing a worrying foreign influence into British foreign policy.

Hanover was a bit-player in the Great Northern War. This was essentially a contest between Russia and Sweden. Hanover had entered the war on the Russian side and had lofty ambitions for territorial gains. In the days before George's accession, this would have been of little relevance to Britain. Now, however, Hanoverian desires were an important feature of British politics. The Elector of Hanover wanted to seize the ports of Bremen and Verden from Sweden. Hanover had little hope of achieving this by itself. It would need powerful help if it was to succeed. Happily for Hanover, her Elector was also Britain's King and the master of the Royal Navy. Ships from the British fleet were duly despatched to conquer the coveted ports for Hanover. Alas, Hanover proved no more capable of holding these territories than she had been of winning them and more British ships and troops had to be sent to secure them against Swedish attacks.

The Act of Settlement had made it clear that this should not have happened. British blood and British treasure should only have been spent in pursuit of British interests. Instead we found our foreign policy being directed in accordance with Hanoverian ambitions. There was unrest in the country and anger in Parliament. A number of ministers resigned in protest. One of those to hand back the seal of office was Robert Walpole.

Walpole was not opposed to the Hanoverian Succession per se but he did feel that it was being managed badly. He recognised that it was a good thing to have a Protestant ruler but he thought that we were being made to pay too high a price for the privilege.

The 1715 Rising and the Great Northern War had made some question whether we had made a poor deal in appointing a Hanoverian sovereign. The disadvantages of the Hanoverian Succession were beginning to dominate the scene. That was about to change. Walpole and the other sceptics would soon realise that there were circumstances in which a foreign monarch could be good for the development of domestic freedom. They were to see this clearly demonstrated in one of the most significant domestic crises of the eighteenth century: the South Sea Bubble.

If one describes a period of febrile economic activity in which herd instinct took the place of rational thought and in which people enthusiastically dashed into investments that made little sense and carried great risk, you might think back to the pre-2007 City boom. You might just as easily, however, think back to London in the first decades of the 1700s. During those years, the great mercantile companies sought investment from the public in exchange for shares in the profits of the businesses in which they invested.

This was a time of riotously unprincipled capitalism. There was a Del Boy on every street and a Bernie Madoff around every corner. Here was a company with some brilliant new invention, there was a company with privileged access to some wondrous raw material. Perhaps they had developed exclusive contacts in exotic markets or maybe they had the inside track on lucrative Government contracts. Some were legitimate, others not. Many did not even bother with extravagant promises. One enterprising conman asked speculators to invest in "a Company for carrying on an undertaking of great advantage, but no one to know what it is". The audacity of actually putting this out to market almost makes one admire the genius behind it. Moreover, this fraudster knew not to push his luck. He spent a day accepting investments before shutting up shop and sailing off to the Continent.

In contrast to the "undertaking of great advantage", the South Sea Company did have a legitimate operation but, also unlike the undertaking of great advantage, they had no sense of how to quit when they were ahead.

The basis of the South Sea Company was the right to send one ship a year to trade with the Spanish territories in South America. This right had been granted to Britain under the Treaty of Utrecht and it had subsequently been acquired by the South Sea Company. Undoubtedly that right had a value and it should have been the source of a decent income stream. The South Sea Company's directors, however, had bigger plans. They decided to take on a portion of the national debt.

The result of this was to make an investment in the South Sea Company look very attractive indeed. Access to the riches of the South Seas meant that there was the possibility of serious gain while the connection to the National Debt made the investment seem relatively risk-free.

The combination of large returns from a safe investment meant that South Sea Company shares soon became popular. The share price began to creep upwards and rocketed when the Company's directors began to talk up the prospects for South American trade. As the share price soared it took on a life of its own. At the beginning of 1720 the shares had been trading at around £100 each. By August the price had reached £1,000. Egged on by the directors, investors had grossly overvalued the South Sea Company's business. With the stock rising so quickly, however, people did not want to miss out. Many borrowed to invest. In the end, as bubbles do, the South Sea Bubble burst.

By September the stock had fallen back to the £100 mark. If you had bought at the top you had lost a staggering amount. Many speculators were ruined. The large number of bankruptcies had a knock-on effect for banks and other lenders as they were left unable to collect on the loans that they had advanced for the purchase of South Sea shares. The economic cost was tremendous and we may be sure that the personal costs for individuals were just as grave. This was one of the severest crises of the century and it quickly became the dominant political issue of the day. With a country facing an emergency of this magnitude one would have expected the monarch to direct, or at least to supervise, the Government's response.

George, however, was largely absent from the scene. The King had no interest in dealing with this sort of domestic matter. Responsibility therefore devolved on Britain's elected politicians.

Having publicly spoken against certain aspects of the South Sea Company's business and not having been in office at the time of the Government debt deals, Walpole was well placed to take the lead in sorting out the aftermath of the Bubble. He acted decisively.

He confiscated the personal fortunes of the Company's directors and used these funds to repay some of those who had lost out as a result of the Bubble. Then he reorganised the holding of Government debt and transferred some of the Company's assets to the Bank of England. As can often be the case in economic matters, the manner in which the measures were delivered was more important than the measures themselves. Walpole's masterful approach generated confidence that a firm hand was on the tiller and that, in itself, made a powerful contribution to stabilising both the economic and the political situation.

The South Sea Bubble demonstrated and accelerated the transfer of power from King to Ministers and to Parliament. If Walpole had earlier blanched at the costs of the Hanoverian Succession, he would now see that there were also major compensations. The lack of interest shown by a foreign monarch had made it possible for a Member of Parliament to carve out a new role in the British constitution. The Prime Minister would not yet replace the monarch as the chief executive figure in the Government (we would have to wait many years for that) but an elected figure would now have a role of major consequence in the State. Walpole had been appointed First Lord of the Treasury, Chancellor of the Exchequer and Leader of the House of Commons. By the end of the South Sea Bubble crisis his power had grown and was more than the sum of these titles. Indeed, he began to be referred to (not always kindly) by a new and unofficial title: Prime Minister.

There had been chief ministers for centuries but the position created by Walpole was different. Firstly, the fact that the King had largely abandoned the conduct of day-to-day government meant that Walpole had far greater power than his predecessors. Secondly, while Walpole definitely served at the King's pleasure, he had also to command the confidence of the Commons. The development of the Prime Ministerial role necessarily entailed the growth of

Parliamentary power. If the Prime Minister was to stay in office he would have to keep the Commons happy. This came easily to Walpole.

The ablest Parliamentary manager of his time (perhaps of any time), he had an instinctive feel for the levers of power. Patronage and money, favours and threats were deftly and profitably deployed. For the bulk of his premiership he was without an equal in the House of Commons. And his was a long premiership. He was First Lord of the Treasury for over twenty years. He was not animated by any great reforming spirit and he introduced few innovations. He had no enthusiasm for aggressive foreign activity and he did not long to improve the condition of the people. Some of his contemporaries thought him insufficiently patriotic and lacking in ambition for his country. This was unfair. Walpole wanted to avoid war, to allow commerce to thrive, to keep taxes low and to keep the country free from internal disruption. As programmes for government go, Walpole's was a noble effort. He may have been a corpulent, claret-glugging bon viveur but there was much more to him that that. He created the role of Prime Minister and set a high standard for his successors. Sadly for Walpole, in empowering himself, he had also been empowering those who could help choose when his immediate successor should take over. Parliament had seen its influence grow and it was getting restless.

Here was a further consequence of the Hanoverian Succession. The King was only interested in British foreign policy to the extent that this policy was able to aid Hanover. The control of British foreign policy more generally was untended. Parliament picked it up with gusto. MPs wanted Britain to take an active and leading role in world affairs. They wanted to open new markets for British commerce and they wanted to add to the number of Britain's imperial possessions. With these aims in mind they were looking for an excuse for war. In 1731 they found one in Robert Jenkins.

Robert Jenkins was a sea captain commanding a merchantman in the South Atlantic. As we know from our examination of the South Sea Company, Britain was only permitted to send one ship a year to the South Atlantic. Britain's burgeoning economy chafed at this restriction and our trade with South America soon outgrew that one ship; illegal smuggling was rife. Unsurprisingly, the Spanish Government and Spanish merchants were angered by these frequent, flagrant breaches of Britain's treaty obligations. Spanish retaliation was inevitable; when it happened it was Jenkins who bore the immediate brunt. Jenkins' ship was boarded and the Spanish used Jenkins himself to make their point to the British Government. They cut off Jenkins' ear and sent him back to London to tell the British that no more smuggling would be tolerated.

When the story of Jenkins' Ear got about, the country erupted in fury and Parliament was swift to give full vent to that rage. Walpole parleyed with the Spanish and reached a deal with them in the Convention of El Pardo. He thought this Convention would satisfy Parliament; he was mistaken. Parliament wanted war and it was not to be fobbed off: William Pitt (later Earl of Chatham and known to history as Pitt the Elder) said:

> "Is this any longer a nation? Is this any longer an English Parliament, if with more ships in your harbours than in all the navies of Europe; with above two millions of people in your American colonies, you will bear to hear of the expediency of receiving from Spain an insecure, unsatisfactory, dishonourable Convention?[17]"

Pitt, speaking for Parliament as a whole, wanted Britain to get the best deal out of international affairs. The King might not have cared, but Parliament did and they took action to get their way. They pushed Walpole into war and, when the war started to go badly, they

[17] http://www.gutenberg.org/files/10990/10990-8.txt

forced Walpole out of office. Whatever you think of the rights and wrongs of these policies, they certainly show that British liberty expanded as a result of the Hanoverian Succession. Parliament was calling the tune and the Prime Minister was carrying out its wishes. The King (now George II) was not involved. What happened next, however, would show that foreign policy under the Hanoverian Succession was not a one-way street. George may not have been interested in Britain thus far but her entry into the war would change all that.

The War of Jenkin's Ear soon merged into the general European conflict of the War of the Austrian Succession, with Britain on the Austrian side fighting France, Prussia and Bavaria. Hanover was another ally of Austria's. Sadly, however, she had proved rather a feeble one and, after taking an early part in the war, she had been beaten into neutrality. Britain's entry into the war could remedy that state of affairs. With British backing, Hanover could re-enter the fray and redeem her honour. George made it his top priority to secure that backing. On the King's order, the British Government provided significant financial backing to the Hanoverian army. Parliament was aghast.

Pitt and his colleagues had wanted war against Spain on the high seas to defend and advance our trading interests. They had not wanted us to be bogged down in military action on the continent and they certainly did not want us wasting money on the Hanoverian army. Pitt's attack in the Commons was scathing. He asked the bald question: "why should the Elector of Hanover exert his liberality at the expense of Great Britain?[18]" The question needed no answer and he went on to give his own view:

> "It is now too apparent, sir, that this great, this powerful, this mighty nation, is considered only as a province to a

[18] Ibid

> despicable Electorate; and that in consequence of a scheme formed long ago, and invariably pursued, these troops are hired only to drain this unhappy country of its money. That they have hitherto been of no use to Great Britain or to Austria, is evident beyond a doubt; and therefore it is plain that they are retained only for the purposes of Hanover[19]."

At the end of his speech Pitt said:

> "I shall not dwell farther on this unpleasing subject than to express my hope, that we shall no longer suffer ourselves to be deceived and oppressed: that we shall at length perform our duty as representatives of the people: and...show, that however the interests of Hanover have been preferred by the ministers, the Parliament pays no regard but to the interests of Great Britain[20]."

Here was his point. The King still had ultimate control over the appointment of British ministers and the King cared chiefly for Hanover. This created an incentive for ministers to pander to the King's German interests in order to secure power in Britain. This danger had been foreseen when the Act of Settlement had first been suggested. In the Austrian War, it had now come to pass. Was this a fundamental and incurable flaw in the Hanoverian Succession or had poor management allowed an unnecessary problem to emerge? In order to answer that question we should look beyond the War of the Austrian Succession to the next European conflict: the Seven Years' War.

The Seven Years' War involved fighting in Europe, America and India, and so has a claim to be the first "world war". It would turbo-charge Britain's imperial power, secure Pitt's place in the pantheon of British heroes and demonstrate how the shared monarchy of

---

[19] Ibid

[20] Ibid

Britain and Hanover worked in practice. The man charged with leading Britain through these stormy years was none other than William Pitt the Elder.

After his intemperate and anti-Hanover speeches during the War of the Austrian Succession, Pitt was the last man in Britain whom George would want leading the war effort but he was also the only man in Britain who would be acceptable to Parliament and the country. George's hand was forced and Pitt was appointed to head the Government. Britain was lucky to have him.

Winston Churchill in the third volume of his *A History of the English-Speaking Peoples* wrote thus of Pitt:

> "Nothing like it had been seen since Marlborough. From his office in Cleveland Row Pitt designed and won a war which extended from India in the East to America in the West. The whole struggle depended upon the energies of this one man. He gathered all power, financial, administrative, and military, into his own hands...[I]n the execution of his military plans Pitt had a sure eye for choosing the right man. He broke incompetent generals and admirals and replaced them with younger men upon whom he could rely: Wolfe, Amherst, Conway, Howe, Keppel, and Rodney. Thus he achieved victory[21]."

And what a victory, or rather, victories.

General Wolfe won Canada for Britain when he captured Quebec at the Battle of the Plains of Abraham. Generals Clive and Eyre Coote did likewise in India, winning the Battle of Plassey and seeing off the siege of Madras. The French had been driven both from North America and from India. The story was the same on the high seas.

---

[21]Churchill, Winston S, *A History of the English-Speaking Peoples*, Weidenfeld & Nicolson 2002, Page 123

The French fleet was given a bloody nose at the Battle of Lagos and then comprehensively smashed at the Battle of Quiberon Bay. 1759 was a particularly successful year and one contemporary wrote, "Our bells are worn threadbare with ringing for victories." That great naval song *Heart of Oak* also refers to 1759 when it says:

Come, cheer up, my lads, 'tis to glory we steer,
To add something more to this wonderful year;

Heart of Oak also says:

We still make them feel and we still make them flee,
And drub them ashore as we drub them at sea,
Then cheer up me lads with one heart let us sing,
Our soldiers and sailors, our statesmen and king.

It is hard to imagine a modern popular song in which politicians are ranked as heroes alongside soldiers, sailors and the monarch. However, when they sang of statesmen, the British people were doubtless thinking of Pitt and they were happy to count him as a hero.

Pitt was the founder of Patriot politics. His heart beat with Britain's and a passion for his country's honour drove his every act. He wanted Britain to be free, strong and prosperous but, more than that, he wanted Britain to be the world's foremost power. In his day and in his mind that meant that Britain should enjoy command of the seas and possess a large colonial empire. It also meant, by logical extension, that no other country should do so. The majority of the British people concurred and, together, they largely achieved their aim. The Seven Years' War, however, was not just about empire and the high seas.

France was principally a military power in Europe and, if France was to be fully defeated, she would have to be defeated on the battlefields of Europe. British troops, as we have seen, were largely occupied in Canada and India. We would need someone else to do the bulk of the heavy lifting in Europe. Pitt's mind turned to Prussia. As we will see, thinking of Prussia soon meant thinking of Hanover.

There was no doubt that Prussia would wish to fight France, but Pitt could not be certain of how committed she would prove. One thing was for sure, if her left flank were exposed, she could well drop out of the war. The best way of securing Prussia's left flank was for Hanover to play a full part on the British/Prussian side. However, as one German ally pointed out, Hanover was in no position to fight independently. If she were to enter the war she would have to be given the necessary funds.

The logic was unavoidable. Britain could not beat the French without beating them in Europe; the French would not be beaten in Europe without the Prussians staying in the war; the Prussians would not stay in the war unless Hanover was prepared to fight; and Hanover would not be prepared to fight unless Britain paid for it to do so. Not only was this logic unavoidable, it was potentially very uncomfortable for Pitt. It seemed that his attitude during the War of the Austrian Succession had come back to haunt him. Back then he had denounced the Hanoverian subsidies in the strongest terms. Everyone thought that, if he himself now had to pay such subsidies, it would undermine his position as a patriot politician. Pitt, however, was a subtler operator than that. He detected a helpful nuance in the Hanoverian Succession.

It was not true that paying subsidies to Hanover would inevitably mean subordinating Britain's interests to those of a "despicable Electorate". If the result of the subsidies was that Prussia fought the French then this was very much in Britain's interests and we would pay them regardless of who sat on the Hanoverian throne. The point was not that Hanover could not receive British money; the point was that Hanover should only receive British money as payment for advancing British interests. In Pitt's view this had not happened in the War of the Austrian Succession.

During the Austrian War, Pitt had observed that the Hanoverian soldiers for which Britain was paying had "marched to the place most distant from the enemy, least in danger of an attack, and most strongly fortified"[22]. It had therefore seemed to Pitt that the troops in question had actually "left their own country for a place of greater security" and, bearing that in mind, Pitt had questioned whether "the money of this nation can not be more properly employed than in hiring Hanoverians to eat and sleep". There would be no repetition of that in the Seven Years' War. If Britain were to provide the bucks she would demand some serious bang in return. According to one of Pitt's colleagues, "Mr Pitt is strongly for...sending an order" to the Hanoverians commanding them "to fall upon the French immediately" but "Mr Pitt declares against giving...[a] single farthing from hence till the troops are in activity".

There, in a nutshell, is the point about managing the Hanoverian Succession. Not everything that Britain could do for Hanover would be against the British interest. It made sense to support the Hanoverian war effort. Indeed, the money was extremely well spent. The British troops deployed in Europe and the German allies for which Britain paid did sterling work. Pitt himself said that "America was won in Germany". Pitt had never argued that Hanover should not be supported; his view was simply that she should not get a better deal just because she happened to share a monarch with Britain. The Hanoverian Succession did bring drawbacks and there were question marks over our sovereignty but the position was not an absolute one. A determined Prime Minister (and few have been more determined than Pitt) could stand firm and make sure that Britain's resources were only used where they would further

---

[22]http://www.classicpersuasion.org/cbo/chatham/chat06.htm

Britain's interests and that Hanover could not profit unfairly from her British connection.

So where does this leave us? The Hanoverian Succession saved Britain from a tyrannical, pro-French, Roman Catholic dynasty. The first two Hanoverian monarchs were neglectful of Britain's domestic affairs and created a vacuum in the British Constitution into which a Parliament and the Prime Minister could step. As a direct result of the Hanoverian Succession the publicly accountable elements of the State would wax in power and the democratic freedoms of the British people would grow alongside (albeit slowly and from a low base). Moreover, while the King was still the country's chief executive, the Prime Minister had more power than any subject had previously held and this power could be put into the hands of the person best suited to deploy it. Britain benefitted greatly from the efforts of Walpole and, even more, from the work of Pitt the Elder; this would not have been possible if the Hanoverian Succession had not allowed scope for the emergence of the Prime Minister.

On the other hand, there were those who could not in honesty call the Georges their Kings. The existence of the Jacobite cause generated a great deal of tension and uncertainty while the Stuart rebellions led to British property being destroyed and to British lives being lost. Then there was foreign policy. Walpole resigned because he felt that Hanover was using Britain in the Great Northern War and Pitt used all his eloquence to denounce Hanoverian subsidies during the War of the Austrian Succession. Ministers could indeed be tempted to outbid each other in their support for Hanover in order to win the royal favour and, thereby, to gain domestic power. Yet both Walpole and Pitt came to realise that the growth of ministerial power in the domestic sphere was a considerable gain and that, even in foreign policy, Hanover's interests need not be supreme. Ultimately Hanover could be managed and it could be managed by a British Prime Minister who would not have enjoyed the authority that he had unless he had a foreigner for a King.

When we see threats to sovereignty and when we see foreign influence over the deployment of British resources we should be prepared to stand firm. This does not mean that compromises should never be made but it does mean that they should only be made if we get a good deal.

Epilogue

It is worth pausing to recall that the end of the Stuart dynasty was one of the main reasons for the creation of the Kingdom of Britain. Given that much work is still to be done to strengthen the Union between England and Scotland in light of the recent Scottish referendum, it seems worth referring to this separately.

England and Scotland had been linked by the same monarch since 1603 (with a shared period of Cromwellian dictatorship during the Interregnum). There were many reasons why the ties created by the Union of the Crowns came to be seen as insufficient, and why people on both sides of the Border began to want to form a closer alliance and even a Union. The prospect of the Hanoverian Succession, however, forced the pace. If the House of Hanover came to the throne in England while a Stuart succeeded in Scotland, the last few centuries of joint history would be undone. This concentrated minds and, while it was not the only factor that brought about the Union, it was a very important one.

We can now see how quickly the legal concept of the Kingdom of Britain developed into a national idea with a place of honour in the hearts of the British people. The failure of the Jacobites in 1745 shows this neatly.

The Forty Five rising is commemorated in *The Skye Boat Song*, one of the loveliest pieces of music ever written. It tells of how Bonnie

Prince Charlie, defeated and pursued by Government forces, made haste to the Isle of Skye to effect his escape to France. It is fitting that the last Stuart pretender should have quit the British Isles via Skye. For Skye came to represent the disappearance of the cause he wanted to lead.

Bonnie Prince Charlie and his advisers still believed that there was a powerful enmity between the Scots and the English. This thinking led Prince Charles to launch his invasion in Scotland and to retreat to Scotland when the going got tough. His final battle took place at Culloden in Scotland and, in the wake of his defeat, he wanted to rely on the Scots to smuggle him out of the British Isles. If you wanted to find reliable Scots who would be loyal to the last of the Stuarts, it seemed obvious that you should head to that most Scottish of places: to the Isle of Skye.

The Isle of Skye is MacLeod country. The Chiefs of Clan MacLeod have held sway there since the thirteenth century. In 1745 the MacLeod of MacLeod had his stronghold at Skye's Dunvegan Castle (as, indeed, does the current Chief). Few places are more sacred to the magic of Scotland[23]. Where else in the world could you see an original fairy flag? According to legend the Fairy Flag was given to the MacLeods by a fairy queen and has the power to win three battles by being unfurled in the face of the enemy (after the third unfurling the magic would be spent). You cannot get much more Scottish than the MacLeods, Dunvegan and Skye and yet even here, the last of the Stuarts received a cold welcome.

Flora Macdonald apart, few on Skye rallied round to help the Bonnie Prince. They saw him as a vagabond usurper determined to upset the peace of the realm, and when they thought of the realm they thought of Britain as well as of Scotland. Like the rest of Scotland,

[23] I should declare a family interest in that my mother is a McLeod.

the MacLeods in 1745 had faced a choice. They could fight for a Scottish king from the House of Stuart or they could fight for a British king from the House of Hanover. Like many in Scotland, the MacLeods chose the latter. In 1745 the Chief of the MacLeods led his forces into battle on the side of the Government against the Jacobites. The support of so Scottish a figure as the MacLeod of MacLeod shows how strong the idea of Britain had grown. Nor was this the last time that the MacLeods would show commitment to the British cause. They were to do so again two centuries later, during the Second World War.

Between 1939 and 1945 MacLeods, alongside other Scots, fought in theatres of war across the world. In doing so they brought the skill and bravery of Scotland to the defence of Great Britain. The most romantic aspect of this is represented not by gallant soldiers but by an offer supposedly made by Flora MacLeod, the chief of the Clan. The story is told that Flora wrote to Winston Churchill telling him that she was prepared, in the event of a German invasion, to go to Dover, to stand on the White Cliffs and to deploy the Fairy Flag.

Happily, Churchill never had to call upon the services of Chief Flora and the Fairy Flag but perhaps the image makes the point well: the Chief of the MacLeods standing on the English shore with a Scottish treasure to defend British freedom. Though resolutely Scottish, the MacLeods have continued to be proudly British.

The Hanoverian Succession helped gift the Kingdom of Britain to the world and the peoples of England and of Scotland lost no time in making it their own. Both peoples have benefitted greatly since. As Great Britain seeks to move forward after the Scottish referendum it is worth remembering the patriotism of Flora MacLeod and the fact that it is possible to be both resolutely Scottish and proudly British.

PART II – INFLUENCE

Leading the fight against Napoleon: Pitt, Nelson, Wellington, Castlereagh

Apsley House was and remains the Duke of Wellington's London residence. It contains a cornucopia of Wellingtonian treasures. One of my favourites is the annotated painting of 1836's Waterloo Banquet. The Waterloo Banquet was an annual dinner given by the Duke of Wellington to honour the senior generals who had fought in the British Army on 18th June 1815. Few of us will attend such distinguished work reunions.

Dressed in scarlet uniforms and with medals and chivalric sashes aplenty, the most senior veterans of the Waterloo campaign would annually transform Apsley's Waterloo Gallery into a British Valhalla. We may be sure that these old warriors attended in high good humour to recall old stories and to remember (perhaps with advantages) the feats of Waterloo. If, at times, the mood became a touch self-congratulatory, well, where was the harm? Were not those who had thrashed Napoleon and saved Europe entitled to pat each other on the back? Certainly their country thought highly of her heroes and was generous with honours. Few have been as comprehensively honoured as Arthur Wellesley.

In addition to being the Duke, the Marquess, the Earl and the Viscount of Wellington, he was also the Marquess and the Baron Douro, a Knight of the Garter, a Privy Counsellor, the Commander-in-Chief of the British Army, the Lord Lieutenant of Hampshire, the Lord Warden of the Cinque Ports, a Fellow of the Royal Society and, at various times, Chancellor of Oxford University, Governor of the Tower of London and Prime Minister. And that was just in Great Britain.

In our enthusiasm to hail one of Britain's greatest figures we sometimes forget the extent to which he was also a European leader held in continent-wide esteem.

Wellington's European honours were on at least as grand a scale as his British ones. The Swedes made him a Knight of the Sword, only to be outdone by the Portuguese who dubbed him a Knight of the Tower and Sword. Not content with this, Portugal also created him Count of Vimeira and Marquess of Torres Vedra, while in Spain he was Duke of Ciudad Rodrigo and a Grandee of the First Class and, in the Netherlands, he became the Prince of Waterloo. The nations of Europe could scarcely have done more to honour the man whom many regarded as an earthly saviour.

There is, however, a richer sign of Wellington's European leadership and it, too, may be found in Apsley House: Wellington's collection of field marshals' batons. Rarely created, field marshal is the senior military rank. With that in mind one would be surprised had Wellington not held it. Batons plural, however, gives one pause for thought. Wellington was not only a British field marshal. He was also a field marshal in the armies of Austria, Hanover, the Netherlands, Portugal, Prussia, Spain and Russia.

Whether or not it is ever reasonable to speak of one man as a continent's saviour, it is no more than the truth to say that, at some of Europe's most critical moments, Wellington had been its most important leader. He had been given the top rank in the armies of the seven continental European countries as a symbol of that leadership. He was the only Briton to be so honoured, but a number of other Britons also played leading roles in the struggle against Napoleon and in the efforts to rehabilitate European politics following Bonaparte's exile to St Helena.

Four men with claims to be among, respectively, Britain's greatest Prime Ministers (Pitt the Younger), admirals (Nelson), generals

(Wellington) and Foreign Secretaries (Viscount Castlereagh) took charge and marshalled the forces of the rest of Europe against France.

One must be wary of overstatement. The Europeans were essential too. Without Russia (the country as much as the nation), Napoleon might have ruled Europe for decades notwithstanding Britain's efforts. Despite the absence of British troops and British generals, the anti-French forces defeated Napoleon at the Battle of Leipzig and exiled him to Elba and, had they kept better guard of him, there would have been no Waterloo. Though Wellington was sometimes slow to acknowledge the fact, Waterloo itself might have had a very different ending indeed had Blucher not led the Prussians to our aid; Britain could not have beaten France without her European allies.

Nevertheless, it is equally clear that those European allies could not have beaten France without Britain. This was the nature of a new relationship with Europe. Britain's new role was to fight with European allies as part of an emphatically European cause of which we were usually the de facto leaders. The European cause in question was the defeat of Revolutionary and Napoleonic France. No easy business.

France was Europe's leading power. She started with many natural advantages in terms of population size and national wealth but there was more to it than that. Her armies had established and maintained high standards. Her merchants had competed in economies across the known world. Paris was a leading light of European civilisation. Her recent kings had squandered many of the government's resources but the country was still a force to be reckoned with. More than that, France was soon unified by the knowledge that she had to stand alone against a Europe that was determined to bring her down. France was fighting for her very existence.

In overthrowing and executing Louis XVI, France had spat in the face of monarchical Europe. Across the Continent, kings and noblemen feared for their futures. If it could happen in France, they reasoned, why should it not happen in their countries and on their estates? This prospect galvanised the rest of Europe into action. They were determined to pre-empt other revolutions by discrediting the prototype. If they successfully invaded France, crushed the revolution, punished the regicides and restored the Bourbons it would serve as a warning to would-be revolutionaries elsewhere in Europe that their chances of success were limited. Europe's ruling classes saw this as a struggle for their way of life. They were playing for the highest stakes and would be prepared to throw everything they had at the French. The French did not doubt this and they were equally aware that, if France's enemies prevailed, reprisals would be bitter. Knowing this united the French, put fire into the hearts of their soldiers and drew the whole country into a unified national cause.

However, if both sides were passionately committed to their respective causes, only the French benefitted from any unity as result. The Allies struggled to put aside their various differences. Each Allied power had a monarch and a military establishment which valued its own freedom of action and which was loathe to submit to any other authority. They were also reluctant to share plans, resources or sacrifices. They were not, therefore, able to muster their whole might for the struggle against the French. And, as they years went on, some even ceased to be keen to do so.

Prussia, Russia and Austria, for instance, often seemed more interested in trying to seize chunks of Poland and other territories and each of the Allies wanted to score minor victories at the expense of the others. They all had one eye on positioning themselves for the post-victory settlement; this meant that they were working less hard on achieving the necessary victory and that victory was slipping ever further away. This was particularly true after Napoleon Bonaparte took charge of the French State and began to dazzle the world with his military brilliance. The rest of Europe needed to up its game. It needed leadership – British leadership.

This was clear to the British Prime Minister, Pitt the Younger. After a period out of office, Pitt had returned to power on 10 May 1804 and he found his country once again at war with France. Pitt was determined to prosecute this war with all the vigour it required. France had fought and smashed the two European coalitions that had faced her so far. This did not bode well but Pitt was not to be put off. He would mastermind the Third Coalition.

Alas, this Third Coalition would not itself defeat Napoleon (Europe would have to wait until the Seventh Coalition for that), but the Third Coalition was a necessary prerequisite of eventual Allied victory. The Third Coalition kept up the pressure on Napoleon, preserved Allied opposition to the Emperor and saw an Allied victory in the greatest naval battle of the Napoleonic Wars. These were considerable achievements and they show how important British leadership had become – for the Third Coalition would not have come about without Pitt and it would have been largely bereft of victory without Nelson.

We should turn first to the Coalition's formation. Pitt lost no time in getting started. He knew the players that he would need on his team: Austria, Prussia, Russia and a number of smaller powers (such as Sweden) would all be essential if victory was to be turned from pipedream to realistic prospect. He needed to win them all and he knew how best to go about persuading them. This was not a time for romantic appeals to monarchical unity, nor even for heartfelt condemnations of Gallic barbarity. What was needed was cash. And lots of it. Then as now, wars were expensive and Britain was a wealthy country. If the Allies were to fight, they would have to be paid to do so. Pitt saw that the price would be worth paying and duly opened the national chequebook.

Sweden was first. For £80,000 the Swedes committed troops to a fresh anti-France coalition. Next came Russia. As a bigger prize and with more to offer, the Russians obviously came with a larger price tag (a cool £3 million) but she too agreed to join with Britain against Napoleon. Pitt's eyes then turned to Austria. The Austrians were initially rather stand-offish and Pitt's cajoling made little progress until the French invasion of Italy concentrated minds in Vienna. This, coupled with the temptation of their own £3 million subsidy, brought the Austrians into the Third Coalition.

Thus far, the formation of the Third Coalition is a shining tribute to Pitt and to Britain. Thanks to Britain's efforts the anti-French European powers, which had been defeated in the Wars of both the First and the Second Coalitions, were being given another chance. Pitt was within inches of forming a coalition with the combined power to overrun France. All he needed was to get Prussia on side and he could start planning a victory tour of Paris. But Prussia, sadly, let him down.

Relations between Russia and Prussia had been poor for years and circumstances were not yet severe enough for Prussia to overcome her anti-Russian sentiment. This doomed the Third Coalition even before it started. The absence of the Prussians at the Battle of Austerlitz made it inevitable that the Austrians and Russians would be defeated and that, following that battle, Austria would be knocked out of the war. True, this belatedly brought Prussia into the war as part of the Fourth Coalition but, as this Coalition was without Austria, its prospects were no better than those of the Third Coalition. During the War of the Fourth Coalition, Prussia lost half its territory to France and, having lost the support of both Austria and Prussia, Russia also made peace with France.

For all this, however, it would be a mistake to label the Third Coalition an unimportant failure. Without it, Napoleon would have had more time to consolidate his power in France and further to improve the quality of his military forces. The Third Coalition denied him this time. Moreover, the struggle to rid Europe of Napoleon was a marathon, not a sprint, and each stage built upon the last – the Third Coalition was a link in the chain and, as such, was essential to ultimate victory. Not only that, but the War of the Third Coalition played host to one truly outstanding Allied success: the Battle of Trafalgar.

Trafalgar has taken on an almost legendary quality and it was of vital importance. In the short term it freed Britain from the threat of French invasion and limited France to mainland Europe – any wider ambitions were utterly curtailed. Longer-term, this was the battle that secured Britain's command of the seas for over a century. Pedants like to remind us that the song's original text contains the exhortative "Rule Britannia, Britannia rule the waves", but after Trafalgar, there was nothing inaccurate in the misquote: "Rule Britannia, Britannia rules the waves".

On 21 October 1805 twenty-seven ships from the Royal Navy met a larger Franco-Spanish fleet off Cape Trafalgar. The names of the British ships present that day are a thrilling testament to Britain's martial spirit. The British Fleet included Temeraire, Leviathan, Conqueror, Britannia, Agamemnon, Ajax, Orion, Minotaur, Spartiate, Defiance and Thunder. Most famous of all, of course, was the Victory. We can see Nelson pacing decks of the Victory and we can hear him instructing his signaller to issue last battle orders to the Fleet. Nelson's bond with his sailors was a personal one so it is easy to understand that his original order was for the signal to be "Nelson confides that every man will do his duty". Under the circumstances he readily accepted a suggestion that the flagship could presume to speak for the country and that the word "England" should be substituted for "Nelson". The final piece of editing came when the signalman explained that there was no easy signal for "confides" and that "expects" might be better as it would not have to be spelt out letter by letter. Thus the famous signal "England expects that every man will do his duty" was sent to the fleet and gifted to history.

Final orders having been given, battle could commence. This, however, would be unlike almost every other naval battle either fleet had seen. For centuries, nautical warfare had involved the rival fleets forming up in parallel lines and blasting their cannons at each other until there was a victor. Nelson had other plans. His innovative approach was to divide his fleet in two and attack the enemy line in perpendicular fashion. This confused the opposing admirals and helped give the early advantage to Nelson's ships. Nevertheless, much brave fighting was to be required before the battle would be won.

The Victory led the British Column into the enemy line and bore the immediate brunt of Franco-Spanish defence. Indeed, at one point in the battle the Victory's mast locked with that of a French vessel and her cannon fell silent as the gunners came on deck to repel French boarding parties. Happily, the Temeraire soon came to Victory's aid as did a number of other British ships and the battle began to turn in our favour. The Royal Navy captured twenty-two enemy vessels and lost none of her own.

Nelson, fearless to the last, did not hesitate to share the dangers of battle and was shot while directing affairs from the deck of his flagship. Taken below, he lived just long enough to learn of his victory and to be able pronounce his last words in all honesty: "Thank God I have done my duty".

"England expects", Britain's command of the seas, the designation of 21st October as Trafalgar Day and the naming of one of Britain's most important public spaces as Trafalgar Square are among the legacies of the Battle of Trafalgar. It was and remains Britain's most celebrated naval victory. But there is more to it. It had a wider, European aspect that was crucial at the time but which has become forgotten over the years.

Less famous than his last battle signal, but at least as significant to the man, was Nelson's Prayer. On the morning of the battle Nelson wrote:

> "May the great God, whom I worship, grant to my country and for the benefit of Europe in general, a great and glorious victory: and may no misconduct, in anyone, tarnish it: and may humanity after victory be the predominant feature in the British Fleet.
>
> For myself Individually, I commit my life to Him who made me and may His blessing light upon my endeavours for serving my Country faithfully. To Him I resign myself and the just cause which is entrusted to me to defend.
>
> Amen Amen Amen"

Unquestionably Nelson and his fleet fought chiefly for Britain but, as Nelson's Prayer makes clear, they were also fighting "for the benefit of Europe in general".

This point was made even more clearly a few weeks later at the Lord Mayor's Banquet in the City of London. The City of London en fête is always a fair sight to behold but, with the news of Trafalgar still fresh in the air, this was a particularly jubilant evening. Cheering Londoners stopped Pitt's carriage on Cheapside and discharged his horses so that they could carry the Prime Minister to the Guildhall. At the dinner itself, Pitt was the hailed as hero of the hour and was toasted by the Lord Mayor not just as the saviour of Britain but as "the Saviour of Europe". Pitt's reply was masterful:

"I return you many thanks for the honour you have done me; but Europe is not to be saved by any single man. England has saved herself by her exertions, and will, as I trust, save Europe by her example.[24]"

Here truly was the new approach to Europe. It had become our role to offer the leadership that Europe needed to free herself from the menace of her enemies. Pitt had shown this leadership by forming and funding the Third Coalition. Now Nelson had shown dramatic leadership on the high seas. As Pitt's remark quoted above points out, he, Nelson and Britain as a whole had also shown leadership by example. True, Prussia's failure to rally to the cause meant that Europe let Pitt down and that the Third Coalition was not crowned with the victories for which Pitt had hoped. The Third Coalition had, however, brought victory that much closer and, when victory finally came it would be won by British and European forces acting under the leadership of another great British hero: the Duke of Wellington.

Wellington had proved himself a European commander in the Peninsular Campaign. This campaign, termed the "Spanish Ulcer" by Napoleon, drained the French of much-needed resources while also being good PR for the Allies as the succession of French Marshals sent to tackle Wellington were each in turn sent packing. While British arms won great victories in the Peninsular, they did so alongside the Spanish and Portuguese. The Spanish guerrillas were invaluable while Portuguese troops were actually integrated into the British Army to form an Anglo-Portuguese force. Already Wellington was used to giving orders to foreign troops and relying on them to carry them out. This would serve him well on 18th June 1815.

---

[24] Quoted in Hague, William, *William Pitt the Younger*, HarperCollinsPublishers, 2004, Page 565

It is impossible to read accounts of Waterloo without being awed by the gallantry of the combatants. This was true of all the armies involved and of soldiers of every rank. Taking the higher echelons first, a glance at the casualty list shows that the commanders at Waterloo were not armchair generals in chateaux behind the lines. The generals were in the thick of the fighting. On the British side Generals Ponsonby and Picton were both killed at the head of their troops and Lord Uxbridge had his leg blown off. Uxbridge had been next to Wellington at the time and it was also next to Wellington that several of the Duke's ADCs were killed. It is remarkable that Wellington himself survived. This bravery was also a feature of the French high command.

While Napoleon's haemorrhoids kept him out of the saddle and, while he was therefore less exposed to danger than he might otherwise have been, his Marshals more than made up for this. Marshal Ney, for example, had five horses shot under him and led a valiant, though ultimately futile, cavalry attack on the allied infantry. Those in the lower ranks, too, proved themselves to be made of the toughest stuff. Perhaps the clearest sign of this was the Imperial Guard's attack on the British frontline.

One of Napoleon's favourite tactics was to form his crack troops into a column and order them to make a frontal attack on the enemy. Considered as a unit, such a column was a powerful destructive force. For many of the individuals involved, on the other hand, it was a different story. The men at the front of the column were practically on a suicide mission. It took great guts to carry out this manoeuvre. That said, it also took great guts to stand against it.

The column was a terrifying sight. Those in the defenders' front rank saw a vast array of France's finest soldiers advancing relentlessly towards them. Such French columns had often been successful in breaking through their opponents' lines. Napoleon reckoned that the British would crumble before it. Napoleon had underestimated the British soldier.

Napoleon's generals had tried to warn him, telling him of the bravery of the British infantry and of the skill with which Wellington deployed his troops. The top ranks of the French army warned the Emperor that, whatever success he had enjoyed when using this tactic against other enemies, no French column could break the British line. So it proved. In the end the great courage of the French Imperial Guard came up against the even greater courage of the British Foot Guards, and the French were forced to retreat. If Napoleon had underestimated the bravery of the British Army he had also underestimated the generalship of their commander. As Napoleon's generals had told him, Wellington knew how to deploy his troops.

Wellington had skilfully placed many of his soldiers on a reverse slope so that Napoleon did not know the true size of the British position until it was too late. In the end Napoleon (though clearly a great general) and the French Army (though undeniably a fine fighting force) were not quite the equals of their British equivalents. However, despite the central importance of the British and French armies, Waterloo was not a rerun of Agincourt; there was more to it than us versus the French.

While the British Foot Guards played a vital role in repulsing the Imperial Guard, they did so alongside their German and Dutch allies. The German influence was also felt at two of Waterloo's other crux points: La Haie Sainte and Hougoumont. At the beginning of the battle, La Haie Sainte was in the hands of the King's German Legion. These bold Hanoverians held out for hours and were only finally ousted when they had almost run out of men and had completely run out of ammunition. Their efforts tied up French resources that could have been used elsewhere. At Hougoumont (the possession of which was an absolute requirement of winning the battle) troops from the Brunswick and Nassau fought valiantly against superior numbers. Hougoumont was ultimately a triumph for the British Guards divisions but it does not lessen the scale of their efforts to say that the German forces were essential too. Nor were those the only Germans of note.

Particularly important were the Prussians. Marshal Blucher led his troops onto the field to aid Wellington in the nick of time. Their numbers were large, their quality high and, after a recent defeat at the Battle of Ligny, their appetite for thrashing the French was voracious. They turned the tide decisively.

After the battle, Wellington and Blucher met at a farmhouse called La Belle Alliance. La Belle Alliance had been Napoleon's headquarters and Blucher thought that it would be a suitable name for the battle. Wellington was unimpressed and exercised his prerogative to name the battle as he saw fit; and the Battle of Waterloo was written into the history books. No one, not even Blucher, could dispute Wellington's right to name the battle. His leadership and personal courage had been of the first order and it had been Wellington's British troops which had defeated Napoleon's Imperial Guard. Blucher, however, could be forgiven for thinking that La Belle Alliance had a nice ring to it. Overall, it had been a coalition victory. Wellington and the British had led a disparate collection of armies to a collective, European victory.

The Duke's task was made easier by the fact that, on the battlefield, all the parties in the Coalition shared the same aim: to beat the French. When it came to settling peace terms this unity would evaporate. The post-Waterloo peace talks would establish the foundations of European diplomacy for the next century. Had the Continentals been left to their own devices those foundations would have been shaky indeed; it was thanks to British leadership that they were built with enough solidity that a general European war would not come about until 99 years after Waterloo.

The Prussians, the Russians and the Austrians arrived at the Congress of Vienna greedy to nab their shares of the spoils. The Prussians wanted to seize chunks of French territory and to gain control of Saxony. The Russians had their eyes on Poland while Austria wanted Bavaria. Austria lost out on Bavaria, it is said, because its representative overslept after a tiring night with one of his mistresses and missed the relevant meeting. Energy-sapping nocturnal activities could not be relied upon to solve all the Congress' problems. The other territorial claims were only settled after much diplomacy and with threats of renewed war. It was Castlereagh, Britain's Foreign Secretary, who kept everyone in line. He knew that a punitive peace in which France suffered excessively would only store up trouble for the future. He also knew that dangerous resentments might be caused if one or two Great Powers seemed to profit more than the others. Eventually his policy won out and the settlements agreed in the various treaties amounted to a stable balance between the various interests. The nineteenth century could very easily have descended into decades of wars over the post-Napoleonic settlement of the Continent. That it did not is due, very largely, to the efforts and skill of Britain's Foreign Secretary.

Our roles in the Revolutionary and Napoleonic Wars are not always spelt out clearly. Of course we won and, in doing so our soldiers, sailors and statesmen won themselves very considerable glory, but we won at the head of European coalitions. We were not simply anti-French, we were pro a stable Europe. Europe could never have defeated Napoleon, much less secured a largely pacific nineteenth century, without Britain. The Third Coalition failed due to a lack of European support and the Prussians, Brunswickers, Nassaus and Hanoverians would have been smashed at Waterloo without the British. In both cases it was Britain that led the way, relying on Europe to follow wholeheartedly. Sadly she does so all too seldom, but when Europe falls into line behind Britain she tends to do very well out of it.

Championing Europe's underdogs: Palmerston

Not all Foreign Secretaries have deserved to be described as diplomats. Take George Brown, Foreign Secretary in Harold Wilson's Government. He was a man with a well-known fondness both for the bottle and for the fairer sex and he caused us some embarrassment abroad. The story is told that, while under the influence at a state dinner in Peru, his eye came to rest upon a tall, elegant figure in a long red dress. After dinner, the band struck up and Mr Brown darted over to ask for a dance. The tall, elegant figure in the long red dress appeared somewhat affronted and turned him down. Crestfallen, Brown asked why. He was told that there were three reasons: "Firstly, you're drunk; secondly this isn't a waltz, it's the Peruvian national anthem; and thirdly I'm not a woman, I'm the Cardinal-Archbishop of Lima". Alas, the story appears to be untrue but it has been told often enough to serve as a warning of how easy it is to cause offence to foreigners.

Lord Palmerston would never have asked a prelate for a dance but he was certainly known not to care too highly for the opinions of non-Brits. One French diplomat tried to wheedle his way into Palmerston's good books with the line "If I were not a Frenchman, I should wish to be an Englishman". Palmerston had no interest in meeting the poor chap halfway. "If I were not an Englishman", he replied, "I should wish to be an Englishman."

Palmerston is a near-legendary figure. As we will see, he was a dedicated champion of British interests and was not afraid to interfere in the internal affairs of other countries or to engage in gunboat diplomacy where needed. As we will also see, however, this single-minded commitment to Britain was very much to Europe's benefit. Britain was the leading "constitutional" (as opposed to dictatorial) state and the pursuit of British interests generally meant advancing the constitutional interest elsewhere in Europe. It also meant seeking to preserve peace by giving firm rebukes to potentially aggressive foreign powers. Palmerston was not only the man Britain needed, he was also the man Europe needed.

He adopted a work-hard-play-hard approach to life. Once, as a young man, he had the honour of an appointment with the Duke of Wellington but at the disagreeable hour of 7.30am. Someone asked him "Why, Palmerston, how will you keep that engagement?" Palmerston replied that it would be "the easiest thing in the world. I shall keep it the last thing before I go to bed". For most of us an appointment at 7.30am would be the first appointment of that day and not the last of the preceding day; of course, the nature of Palmerston's nocturnal activities is open to question. Very possibly, he would have spent the night working hard in his study but, equally, he may have been engaged elsewhere. Not for nothing was Lord Palmerston sometimes called Lord Cupid. He was quite the ladies' man and had a string of affairs. Perhaps the clearest sign of his success with the fairer sex was his membership of Almack's Club.

Almack's was one of the few London Clubs that was open to both sexes. Originally the new male members had to be elected by existing female members and vice versa but, by Palmerston's time, the control of the Club's operation was largely in the hands of its seven aristocratic Lady Patronesses. These ladies ran the place with a collective iron will. They kept the membership rigorously exclusive. To become a member was to be accepted in the top rank of London society. Even then, however, you had to meet the Lady Patronesses' exacting standards. The dress code, for instance, specified knee breeches for men and when the Duke of Wellington arrived in less formal leg-wear the porter told him that "Your Grace may not be admitted wearing trousers". The victor of Waterloo was forced to seek his evening's entertainment elsewhere. Misbehaviour could even see members face the shame of expulsion. Referring to the "List" of members and to Almack's weekly Wednesday balls, a contemporary poet wrote:

"*All on that magic List depends;*

Fame, fortune, fashion, lovers, friends;

'Tis that which gratifies or vexes

All ranks, all ages, and both sexes.

If once to Almack's you belong,

Like monarchs you can do no wrong;

But banished thence on Wednesday night,

By Jove, you can do nothing right.[25]"

Social climbers lobbied the Lady Patronesses aggressively. Palmerston had no need to do so. Not only was he a third viscount of distinguished lineage but, more importantly, he had, it was widely supposed, bedded three of the seven Lady Patronesses. His busy social calendar and frequent amorous adventures told of a restless, buccaneering spirit. Happily, Palmerston carried that with him into Government.

He had one of the longest ministerial careers in our history but this is not the place to assess the entirety of his record. Here we shall focus on his time as Foreign Secretary. During his tenure of that office, Palmerston looked out at a deeply divided Europe.

The continent was split into constitutional and autocratic states. In the autocratic camp were Austria, Prussia and Russia. These formidable powers were ruled by dictatorial monarchs still preaching the Divine Right of Kings. They were fearful of popular

---

[25] http://www.janeausten.co.uk/almacks-assembly-rooms/

participation in Government and declined to allow their peoples much in the way of personal freedoms. Nor were they keen for democracy (even of a limited, eighteenth-century kind) to be practised beyond their realms; after all this could only be a bad example to agitating reformers at home. The autocratic states were different from and opposed to the constitutional states.

Of course, we should be wary of reading too much into the word "constitutional". It is a highly relative term. Even in constitutional countries, such as Britain, the old ruling class still held sway. Despite this, constitutional states were not absolute monarchies and they were home to an evolving sense of liberty. Britain was the leading constitutional state. This gave us a natural set of allies and a corresponding collection of enemies. Britain's role was to advance the interests of the constitutional side while denying victories to the autocrats. Palmerston gives us his own account of his policy here:

> "The independence of constitutional States, whether they are powerful, like France or the United States, or of less relative political importance, such as the minor States of Germany, never can be a matter of indifference to the British Parliament, or, I should hope, to the British public. Constitutional States I consider to be the natural Allies of this country and whoever may be in office conducting the affairs of Great Britain, I am persuaded that no English Ministry will perform its duty if it be inattentive to the interests of such States.[26]"

This was soon put to the test. Two European states were up for grabs: Portugal and Spain. In both cases the incumbent ruler had only an unstable hold on power. In Portugal that incumbent was an autocrat (Miguel) while in Spain the serving ruler was a constitutionalist (the young Queen Isabella and her mother,

[26] Quoted Chamberlain, Muriel E, *Lord Palmerston*, GPC Books, 1987,Page 49

Christina, as Regent). Miguel was facing a challenge from a constitutionalist (Maria) while Isabella and Christina were up against an aspirant autocrat (Carlos). Europe split along factional lines. Austria, Prussia and Russia favoured the status quo in Portugal and a transfer of power in Spain, while Britain and her allies wanted revolution in Portugal and continuity in Spain. Neither side was in a compromising mood. The stakes were high.

Palmerston sprang into action. Recognising that Portugal was a maritime power, he saw at once that the best assistance Britain could offer was the support of the Royal Navy. However, he also recognised that formally to commit these ships would be to risk provoking the autocratic states into war. Palmerston therefore decided on a more covert approach. He would encourage British sailors to break the law by enlisting in a foreign navy (that of Maria) and taking their great skill and experience into service of the Portuguese constitutional revolution. British seamanship proved decisive and Maria's forces smashed those of the autocratic Miguel. Thereafter Miguel's cause was lost and Maria captured Lisbon only a few weeks later. Despite being formally neutral in the matter, Britain had managed to install a constitutional sovereign in Portugal. Palmerston now wished to capitalise on that victory; the autocrats wanted to undermine it – both sides determined to have their way in the next round. In Spain.

Palmerston saw that matters had moved beyond the point at which covert assistance would be any good. Britain would have to show her true colours and formally support a constitutional settlement for the Iberian Peninsula. Palmerston was keen, however, to avoid committing British troops to the defence of Isabella, the constitutional Queen of Spain. Instead he opted for a diplomatic solution that would further the constitutional interest in Spain and safeguard his Portuguese success.

Palmerston struck up a formal alliance between Great Britain, Spain (as long as she was ruled by Isabella) and Portugal (as long as she was ruled by Maria). Realising the strong links that existed between the French Government and Isabella's Spanish supporters, Palmerston was able to bring the French into his alliance. The Quadruple Alliance was born. Constitutionalist sovereigns were guaranteed for Portugal and Spain, formal allies were secured for Britain, and the ambitions of Austria, Prussia and Russia were checked. Palmerston was delighted. He was particularly pleased to have got one over on the Austrians and, referring to the Austrian foreign minister, he gleefully remarked: "I should like to see Metternich's face when he reads our treaty!"[27] Palmerston had given Europe's constitutional states the upper hand.

Palmerston was also expert at crisis management – even when that crisis involved one of our fellow constitutional states. One such crisis was in Belgium.

After Waterloo, the Allies had united Belgium with Holland under the Dutch monarchy. This was not because the Allies felt those two countries would get along famously but because they had wanted a strong barrier against French expansion into the Low Countries. Everyone expected that Belgium would hate being ruled by a Dutch king and so it proved. In 1830 the Belgians rose in revolt, and by 1831 they had their own constitution and their own king. The Dutch had reluctantly accepted Belgian independence but when the Belgians went on to claim the Grand Duchy of Luxembourg, Holland felt it had been pushed too far. The Dutch invaded and occupied Brussels. The Belgians appealed to the British and the French for assistance. We sent a fleet but it was the French Army that drove the Dutch out of Belgium. The problem was that, having accomplished this, the French Army stayed put. A French army in

---

[27] Quoted in Wilson, Harold, *A Prime Minister on Prime Ministers*, Weidenfeld & Nicolson 1977 Page 68

Belgium was precisely what the Belgian–Dutch union had been designed to avoid, and yet here it was. Palmerston came under political fire for abandoning a major gain of Waterloo. He had to think quickly: how could he get the French to withdraw?

It was easy to see how a British protest could provoke a diplomatic incident with consequences out of all proportion to the underlying problem. Palmerston went for a subtler approach. He wrote to the British Ambassador in Paris, making it clear that the French must quit Belgium immediately or face the risk of all-out war. The clever bit was not to send this via a Foreign Office courier but to send it via France's Embassy in London. Palmerston knew that the French would not be able to resist opening the letter (we would have done the same in their place) and that he would therefore be able to get his message across to them directly and loud and clear, but without the French feeling that they were being publicly bullied. The French promptly withdrew from Belgium.

Britain had secured freedom for Belgium and pushed the French out of the Low Countries, and all with one well-directed letter (backed up, of course, by formidable military might). It was a Palmerstonian masterstroke.

Palmerston had been able to have his way in Portugal, Spain and Belgium and he had been able to do so without the official use of British arms. Alas, this was not always possible. Sometimes the gunboats had to be sent and sometimes they had to be used. Take Turkey. Palmerston was committed to upholding the Ottoman Empire. He saw that the collapse of Turkey would see its territories become the scene of a mass scramble on the part of Europe's great powers. Each would try to gain new lands at the expense of the others and the balance of power would be disrupted. That, Palmerston feared, would have only one result – general European war. Palmerston was determined to preserve peace in Europe by preserving the Ottoman Empire. This would not be an easy business.

The Ottoman Empire was largely a facade. The Sultan had little effective power over the realms that nominally accepted him as their lord. Some of his underlings longed to make a legal reality of their practical independence. Mehemet Ali was one such. Ali was Pasha of Egypt. Notionally this meant that he ruled as governor on behalf of the Ottoman Sultan. In fact he was his own man. He had close links with France and French advisers had helped him modernise Egypt and build a powerful army. Ali believed that the Sultan had promised to make him ruler of Syria (another of the Sultan's domains) and, when the Sultan failed to make good on this promise, Ali invaded. The Sultan appealed to Britain and found a ready ally in Palmerston. Not only was Palmerston unhappy about the possibility that Ali would break up the Ottoman Empire, he was concerned that the Pasha would do so under French auspices and that the resulting settlement would favour French interests. This time he found himself on the same side as Austria, Prussia and Russia and, jointly with them, he proposed a compromise.

Palmerston's proposal was that Ali's governorship of Egypt should become an hereditary office that would be his for life and that he could pass on to his son. In exchange for this, Ali would recognise the Sultan's overlordship and call off his troops. If he did not comply, Ali would face war with Austria, Prussia, Russia and Britain. In the past the formation of an alliance, and the threat of the military force represented by such an alliance, had been enough for Palmerston to be able to have his way. Not this time.

The Pasha was stubborn and would not give up his campaign. Palmerston had to back up his diplomacy with force and he did not hesitate to do so. Mehemet Ali was holed up in Acre and Palmerston ordered the Royal Navy to bombard Acre until Ali capitulated. The

Pasha soon came to his senses and, once again, Palmerston's will prevailed.

This was not always the case; Palmerston would not always have his way. He wanted to free the Italian states from Austrian influence but could offer little more than moral support and, while he wanted to aid Sicily in its rebellion against Naples, he found his hands tied. Nevertheless, British policy had been achieved in Portugal, Spain, Belgium and Turkey. Moreover, this had been to the benefit of constitutionalism and of preserving European peace. British interests and the wider European interests were closely aligned and, in ruthlessly serving the former, Palmerston also served the latter. This was true for a large part of Palmerston's career. There were, however, a few exceptions. Palmerston was first and foremost devoted to Britain and Britons, and if helping them out meant trampling on the rights of foreign countries then so be it – as Greece was about to find out.

During the Easter of 1847 there had been an anti-Semitic riot in Athens. Don Pacifico, a Portuguese Jew, was one of the victims and his house had been torched. He appealed to the Greek Government for compensation. The Greeks turned him down. There matters might have rested had it not been for the fact that Don Pacifico had been born in Gibraltar and that, as Gibraltar was British territory, he was a British citizen. Don Pacifico brought his case to Palmerston.

The Greeks had already entered Palmerston's bad books by failing to repay a loan that Britain had advanced them. Now they had compounded this by daring to snub claims of a British citizen. Palmerston was outraged and lost no time in acting on his anger. He already had a fleet in the vicinity and Palmerston swiftly diverted it to Greece. This was not an empty gesture.

Palmerston wrote to Thomas Wyse, Britain's envoy to Greece, and explained what was to happen when the fleet (under Sir William Parker) reached Greece. Palmerston explained that Parker:

> "...should, of course, begin by reprisals; that is, by taking possession of some Greek property; but the King [of Greece] would probably not much care for our taking hold of any merchant property, and the best thing, therefore, would be to seize hold of his little fleet, if that can be done handily. The next thing would be a blockade of any or all of his ports; and if that does not do, then you and Parker must take such other steps as may be requisite, whatever those steps may be. I remember that at one time it was thought that a landing of marines and sailors at some town might enable us to seize and carry off public treasure of sufficient amount. Of course Pacifico's claim must be fully satisfied.[28]"

This was quite an instruction.

The British Foreign Secretary was ordering that the Royal Navy should seize the Greek Navy or, failing that, Greek property, in order to compensate Don Pacifico. Even by the primitive standards of nineteenth-century international law this was outrageous behaviour. Britain was appointing itself judge, jury and executioner. Due legal process in Greece had reached a decision and Britain was preparing unilaterally to set that aside and to seize Greek property to give effect to a revised, British judgment.

As if that were not enough, Palmerston then remembered that the Don Pacifico issue was not his only quarrel with Greece; there was still the outstanding loan to be considered.

Palmerston told Wyse to:

---

[28] http://archive.org/stream/lifeofhenryjohnt01ashliala/lifeofhenryjohnt01ashliala_djvu.txt

> "... intimate to the Greek Government that although we do not this time come to levy the amount due to us on account of the Greek loan, yet we abstain from doing so in order to give them an opportunity of doing the right thing of their own accord; but that we cannot go on requiring the people of this country to pay fifty thousand a year to enable King Otho to corrupt his Parliament, bribe his electors, build palaces, and lay up a stock purse for evil times, which his bad policy may bring upon him.[29]"

The threat was clear. If Greece did not do "the right thing" (i.e. pay up) of its own accord, it would face British military reprisals. The prospect of these reprisals would soon become a very real one. The Royal Navy arrived and blockaded Athens' harbour. With the menace of this fleet hanging over them, Greek resolve was quick to crumble and they agreed to enter negotiations. Britain, of course, had the upper hand and the Greeks would later pay compensation to Don Pacifico (admittedly they paid him less than he had hoped but even Palmerston had come to accept that Don Pacifico's initial claim had been rather inflated).

Some in Britain thought that Palmerston's response had been hugely over the top but Palmerston had no difficulty in defending his conduct. In the Commons debate on the Don Pacifico affair, Palmerston proudly stated "as the Roman, in days of old, held himself free from indignity, when he could say *Civis Romanus sum*; so also a British subject, in whatever land he may be, shall feel confident that the watchful eye and the strong arm of England, will protect him against injustice and wrong"[30]. Some MPs were against him but many in the Commons, and many more in the country,

---

[29] Ibid

[30] Quoted in Wilson, Harold, *A Prime Minister on Prime Ministers*, Weidenfeld & Nicolson 1977 Page 71

would have shouted "hear hear!" until they were hoarse. This was Palmerston at his truest and best.

What can we say of Palmerston? Like Pitt the Elder, he was fired by his determination to uphold the honour and interest of Britain and he was committed to having his way. Happily for Europe, Palmerston's interpretation of the British interest led him to support and secure constitutional government for Portugal and Spain, freedom for Belgium and peace in the Ottoman Empire. Britain was a free and constitutional state and the result of this was that our interests lay in championing freedom and constitutional government elsewhere. Britain was in the right and, as a result, so was our foreign policy. Europe gained much because Britain acted on her principles.

That said, we must not go too far. It was a happy chance that acting on our principles meant working for Europe's good. If (and when) our principles had required Europe to lose out (as in the case of Don Pacifico) then so be it. Britain and British interests should come first. Palmerston himself made the point best and the last words on the matter should go to him:

> I hold that the real policy of England—apart from questions which involve her own particular interests, political or commercial—is to be the champion of justice and right; pursuing that course with moderation and prudence, not becoming the Quixote of the world, but giving the weight of her moral sanction and support wherever she thinks that justice is, and wherever she thinks that wrong has been done. Sir, in pursuing that course, and in pursuing the more limited direction of our own particular interests, my conviction is, that as long as England keeps herself in the right—as long as she wishes to permit no injustice—as long as she wishes to countenance no wrong—as long as she labours at legislative interests of her own—and as long as she sympathises with right and justice, she never will find herself altogether alone.

She is sure to find some other State, of sufficient power, influence, and weight, to support and aid her in the course she may think fit to pursue. Therefore I say that it is a narrow policy to suppose that this country or that is to be marked out as the eternal ally or the perpetual enemy of England. We have no eternal allies, and we have no perpetual enemies. Our interests are eternal and perpetual, and those interests it is our duty to follow. When we find other countries marching in the same course, and pursuing the same objects as ourselves, we consider them as our friends, and we think for the moment that we are on the most cordial footing; when we find other countries that take a different view, and thwart us in the object we pursue, it is our duty to make allowance for the different manner in which they may follow out the same objects. It is our duty not to pass too harsh a judgment upon others, because they do not exactly see things in the same light as we see; and it is our duty not lightly to engage this country in the frightful responsibilities of war, because from time to time we may find this or that Power disinclined to concur with us in matters where their opinion and ours may fairly differ. That has been, as far as my faculties have allowed me to act upon it, the guiding principle of my conduct. And if I might be allowed to express in one sentence the principle which I think ought to guide an English Minister, I would adopt the expression of Canning, and say that with every British Minister the interests of England ought to be the shibboleth of his policy[31].

[31] http://www.gutenberg.org/files/10990/10990-8.txt

Answering the Eastern Question: Disraeli and Salisbury

On 22nd July 1878, the Most Honourable Robert Arthur Talbot Gascoyne-Cecil, third Marquess of Salisbury, knelt before Queen Victoria at Osborne House and was dubbed a Knight of the Garter. Then as now, the Order of the Garter was England's senior order of chivalry.

We know that the Garter was founded by Edward III, but why he chose to name his new order after an item of clothing is more of a mystery. One legend tells of the King dancing with a lady known as Joan, the Fair Maid of Kent, when her garter slipped from her leg. This caused a certain amount of merriment at the party and Edward was appalled to see a lady being made into a figure of fun. He therefore picked up her garter, returned it to her and pronounced "honi soit qui mal y pense" ("shame be to the person who thinks badly of this"). Edward may have been chivalrous but he does not appear to have been particularly modest and, having safeguarded Joan's honour, his mind immediately turned to the ways in which he could commemorate his gentlemanly act. In the end he elected to create a new order of chivalry and to name it after the fallen garter. Fearful that this emblem might just possibly seem a touch trivial, Edward recruited St George as the Order's patron saint. Perhaps this made sense to Edward, for St George, too, had come to the rescue of a damsel in distress (though, as St George had rescued his damsel from a fire-breathing dragon rather than from the social embarrassment of a minor wardrobe malfunction, the parallel was less than exact). Nor do we know whether Joan would have preferred to have laughed off the incident rather than have it immortalised in the founding mythology of an institution that would still be honoured over six hundred years later.

Whatever Joan's private feelings, the Garter has been awarded to England's most distinguished servants ever since. Lord Salisbury knew that. The Cecils had long been accustomed to places at the top of English politics. The first Cecil to receive the Garter had been Elizabeth I's Secretary of State (and later Lord High Treasurer) William Cecil, Lord Burghley. In the intervening years a number of the Earls and Marquesses of Salisbury would be Garter Knights. Even for the country's leading families the Garter did not just come up with the rations but, if the great company of Cecils in the sky were looking down on the scene at Osborne, it would have seemed perfectly natural to them that another Cecil should wear the blue sash of England's highest order by becoming the 771st Knight of the Garter. What might have surprised them a bit was the identity of the man who, moments before, had become the Order's 770th Knight: a Jew with no recorded ancestors of note and few ancestors who had called England home. His breeding, education and early religion marked him out from the rest of the Garter Knights and, indeed, from the rest of contemporary British leaders. As the Jew in question remarked: "To become a K.G. with a Cecil is something for a Disraeli"[32].

Benjamin Disraeli and Lord Salisbury were two very different men.

Disraeli was a figure of style, dash and romance. He won the Suez Canal for England and transformed the Queen of Great Britain into the Empress of India. He led a Government whose social reforms did more than almost all of their predecessors to improve the living conditions of the working classes. One of his greatest triumphs was the Second Reform Act which gave thousands more people the right to vote. Immediately after this Reform had been passed by Parliament, Disraeli went to the Carlton Club where the members toasted him as "the man who rode the race, who took the time, who kept the time and who did the trick". Thereafter he went home to

---

[32] Quoted in Roberts, Andrew, *Salisbury Victorian Titan*, Phoenix 2000 Page 206

find Mrs Disraeli waiting for him with a Fortnum's pork pie and a bottle of champagne. "Really my dear," Disraeli exclaimed, "you're more like a mistress than a wife."[33] It is hard not to warm to Benjamin Disraeli.

Lord Salisbury was an altogether different character. Born into aristocratic purple, there was an almost impenetrable grandeur about him. Once, when Salisbury was Prime Minister, the Duke of Devonshire recommended that Frederick Wills should receive a baronetcy. Wills was a distinguished Member of Parliament and like the rest of his family he was a great benefactor of the City of Bristol. He was also a millionaire and director of the family tobacco company. To many, Wills would have seemed an obvious candidate for a baronetcy. Salisbury only made the appointment with reluctance. Whatever Wills' merits, Salisbury could not ignore his lack of distinguished ancestry and the relative paucity of his social credentials. Having advised the Queen that Mr Wills should become Sir Frederick, he also wrote back to Devonshire saying: "No more tobacconists I entreat you.[34]" Despite this sort of behaviour, Salisbury was an immensely impressive figure.

Salisbury was a genuine intellectual, a committed Christian and a true patriot. He greatly expanded the Royal Navy and presided over a dramatic increase in the scope of Britain's African Empire. He was hugely determined and highly capable.

Salisbury and Disraeli were different but complementary. It was fitting that they were created Garter Knights on the same day in 1878, for they had just returned from Germany having triumphed at the Congress of Berlin.

---

[33] Quoted in Hurd, Douglas and Young, Edward, *Disraeli or The Two Lives*, Weidenfeld & Nicolson 2013 Page 166

[34] Quoted in Roberts, Andrew, *Salisbury Victorian Titan*, Phoenix 2000 Page 662

Bismarck, the German Chancellor, had called the Congress in response to the Treaty of San Stefano which had ended the Russo-Turkish War of 1777–1778. One might reasonably have thought that the Germans, the Russians and the Turks would be the key players. In fact the result was largely stitched up in advance by Salisbury and then driven to its successful conclusion in Berlin by Disraeli. The result was the protection and advancement of British interests and general peace in Europe until 1914. In this chapter we will see how this came about, but first we must examine the background of the quarrel between Russia and the Ottoman Empire.

The Ottoman Empire was the original "sick man of Europe". An incongruous hangover from medieval Europe, it lacked any cohesive sense of unity and was without a strong centre from which the periphery could be controlled. Few nineteenth-century observers believed that the Ottoman Empire was sustainable; but all agreed that its collapse would bring chaos. If Constantinople's rule came to an end the Balkans would become fair game for Europe's Great Powers. Whichever way the various states were carved up, Europe's balance of power would be disrupted and the consequences would be dire. Even if this could not be prevented, many wanted it to be postponed for as long as possible. Britain, in particular, wanted to preserve the status quo. Our rivalry with Russia in Asia required us to keep them from the Mediterranean and the easiest way to achieve this was to keep the Ottoman Empire in place.

Not that this was always easy or agreeable. The Ottoman Empire's Muslim leaders were not a tolerant bunch. The Empire's Christian subjects often suffered greatly and there was much agitation in Britain that we should go to their aid. This was particularly true in the late 1870s. In 1875, the Christians of Bosnia and Herzegovina rose in revolt and they were joined by the Serbs and Bulgarians. Constantinople was not yet quite played out and it still had powerful resources at its disposal. The Christian revolutionaries soon felt the full force of Turkish might. It was a brutal campaign and the British press provided copious coverage of the atrocities that the Turks were committing. Public opinion increasingly swung against the Turks and Gladstone published a pamphlet on *The Balkan Horrors and the Question of the East*. It was only with great difficulty that Disraeli and Salisbury could maintain our traditional pro-Turk stance.

Russia, by contrast, saw an opportunity. How could Holy Mother Russia, the home of the Orthodox Church, stand idly by while Orthodox Christian Slavs were brutally oppressed by their cruel Turkish overlords? Russia was swept by moral and religious outrage. Her ruling class was also swept by the realisation that their long-held desire to seize some of the Sultan's outlying domains and establish themselves on the shores of the Mediterranean could now be carried into fruition under the noble banner of a crusade. Led by the powerful combination of spiritual and earthly motivations, Russia declared war on Turkey.

The Sultan might have been able to oppress his own people with relative ease, but defending his Empire from the attacks of a major military power was another story altogether. The result of the Russo-Turkish War was never in doubt. Turkey got thrashed.

On 3 March 1878 the results of this thrashing were incorporated in the Treaty of San Stefano. The Ottomans ceded Ardahan, Batoum, Bagazid and Kars to Russia and agreed to give independence to Bulgaria, Montenegro, Romania and Serbia. The Bulgaria created at San Stefano was given extensive territory which would have mattered less had not San Stefano given the Russians the right to occupy this "Big" Bulgaria for two years. If San Stefano stood then Russia would dominate the Balkans and have effective control of the Turkish Straits (thus allowing their Navy unfettered access to the Mediterranean).

Lord Salisbury was determined that San Stefano should not stand. He was not alone. Bismarck suggested holding an international summit in Berlin to re-settle the Eastern Question. The question was whether Russia would attend and whether all the Great Powers would be able to reach an acceptable compromise. Salisbury was not happy to leave these points to chance and he swiftly embarked on an ambitious programme of secret diplomacy.

The first stage was to secure the support of an ally. Russian expansion threatened Austria more than Italy, France or Germany and Salisbury thought that she would be in broad agreement that a stable compromise should be reached. He thought, however, that Austria would need a little coaxing if this broad agreement were to be turned into active help so he offered her Bosnia and Herzegovina as a reward should she decide to back Britain in the Berlin negotiations.

Next he had to get the Russians and Turks to agree the outline of a deal. The secrecy of these negotiations allowed the various diplomats to be clear about what they were not prepared to give up, but also to indicate where compromise might be possible –and to do so without any public loss of face. Russia, for instance, would not completely abandon her territorial gains and wanted to keep Batoum and Kars but was prepared to make concessions elsewhere and to agree to a "small" Bulgaria. This would be embodied in a secret Anglo-Russian Convention.

Turkey was in the weaker position but knew that Britain was batting for her. Salisbury told the Turks that, while it would have to accept the permanent loss of some territories, it would have some of its provinces restored and that Britain would act as guarantor of her new borders. In exchange, Turkey would have to enact a series of domestic reforms and cede Cyprus to Britain. Salisbury wanted this to be agreed in an Anglo-Turkish Convention. There was some vacillation in Constantinople but if they thought that they could get a better deal they were wrong. Once the basis of the Anglo-Russian Convention had been agreed, Salisbury told the Turks that if they did not promptly agree to the Anglo-Turkish Convention then they could face the Russians alone and Britain would agree to the carve-up of the Ottoman Empire. Faced with that prospect the Ottomans discovered new enthusiasm for the Anglo-Turkish Convention.

It is unlikely that the settlement contemplated under the Anglo-Russian Convention and in the Anglo-Turkish Convention could have been agreed in a Russo-Turkish Convention. The taste of war was too fresh and the reluctance to deal honestly with an erstwhile opponent was too strong. Left to their own devices, Russia and Turkey would almost certainly have slipped back into war. They needed a third party to mediate. The third party in question had to be someone who had sufficient international clout for both sides to take their intervention seriously. Such powers were few on the ground. Britain, with her foreign policy led by Salisbury, was absolutely essential to the building of the foundations on which the Berlin negotiations would be built. With those foundations complete, the Congress of Berlin could go ahead.

The Congress of Berlin was a triumph for Salisbury and Disraeli. They had to put up with the inconvenience of British officials leaking the terms of some of the pre-Congress agreements but, while embarrassing, this only made clearer the fact that Britain was calling the tune. Austria and Russia tried to weasel out of their agreements with Britain but, in both cases, they received short shrift. Legend has it that when the Russians asked Disraeli to arrange further territorial concessions he simply told them that, if they were unhappy with what they had agreed, they could just say so – but that doing so would mean war with Great Britain. The Russians backed off. Little wonder that, speaking of Disraeli, Bismarck exclaimed: *Der alte Jude, das ist der Mann*!

While sorting things out for Russia and Turkey was the Congress' most important point, Britain also had to deal with the gripes of the bit-players – France, for example. The French were displeased by the prospect of Britain annexing Cyprus. Salisbury knew what to do. France's representative in Berlin was William Waddington. Waddington was a French citizen and had a French mother but his father was English and he had received an English education. Britain has often been represented by men who, like Salisbury, had been educated at Eton and Oxford; more rarely has France been represented by someone who had been at Rugby and Cambridge. Such was the situation in Berlin. Though representing rival countries, the Old Etonian and the Old Rugbeian had no difficulty in reaching a gentlemen's agreement. When Waddington said that the French would be irked by Britain taking Cyprus, Salisbury simply said that France should take Tunisia (another of the Sultan's lands). Neither of them thought to check with the Sultan, much less to consult the Tunisian people. Legally speaking, Tunisia was no more Salisbury's to give than Bosnia and Herzegovina had been. Practically, however, it was a different story. The political map of Eastern Europe, western Asia and northern Africa was being redrawn. And Salisbury was holding the pen.

The Eastern Question had raged for years and had been a fertile source both of diplomatic incidents and military conflicts. Salisbury came as close as anyone to solving it. Standing between the Russians and the Turks he was able to get both to compromise more than they would have wished. Whole countries were at his disposal for the buying of Austrian and French support. Crucially, he was also able to support British interests. Propping up the Ottomans meant that Russia was denied control of the Turkish Straits while the winning of Cyprus strengthened our hand in the Mediterranean.

Like Palmerston, Disraeli and Salisbury were interested in Britain first and in Europe second but, again like Palmerston, their conception of how British interests would best be served was also to Europe's advantage. It was Britain that brokered peace in the Balkans and re-established a workable balance of power that could restore stability in Europe while also defending and advancing British interests.

Palmerston, Disraeli and Salisbury are sometimes caricatured as aggressively pro-British figures, trampling over the rights and interests of others. In fact, under Palmerston as well as under Disraeli and Salisbury, Britain was strong, determined and in the right; Britain benefitted mightily as a result but Europe was a winner too.

PART III: EVER CLOSER UNION?

The European Union

"France and Great Britain shall no longer be two nations, but one Franco-British Union. The constitution of the Union will provide for joint organs of defence, foreign, financial and economic policies. Every citizen of France will enjoy immediately citizenship of Great Britain, every British subject will become a citizen of France[35]."

The above quotation, it may surprise you to learn, comes from a British document. Who do you suppose was behind it? Some croissant-guzzling traitor perhaps? A quisling Francophile wishing to sell his or her country down the river, to give coffee the same rights as tea and to watch as roast beef was kicked aside by frogs' legs? No such thing. This proposal emerged from a meeting chaired by Britain's greatest hero: Winston Churchill.

It was June 1940 and the Nazis were sweeping through Europe. Churchill and the War Cabinet knew that the French were wavering and might at any moment capitulate to the Germans. This was the last thing the British wanted. The Prime Minister realised, however, that if he was going to get the French to commit to the Allied cause, he would have to make his own commitment to the French. The proposed Franco-British Union was the result. Churchill was not ashamed of making this offer.

We all remember his famous exhortation: "let us therefore brace ourselves to our duties and so bear ourselves that, if the British Empire and its Commonwealth last for a thousand years, men will say 'This was their finest hour'". Read the whole speech. A few sentences before the "Finest Hour" Churchill refers to "the historic declaration in which, at the desire of many Frenchmen – and of our

---

[35] Quoted Gibson, Robert, *Best of Enemies: Anglo-French Relations Since the Norman Conquest*, Impress Books Limited, 2004 Page 252

own hearts we have proclaimed our willingness at the darkest hour in French history to conclude a union of common citizenship in this struggle"[36]. This "declaration" went beyond the wildest dreams of today's Euro-enthusiasts. Two nation states were to be abolished by being merged into one. The merged entity would speak with one voice (though perhaps, initially, in two languages) across a wide range of important policy areas.

Taken in isolation, it might seem a little odd that Churchill and his colleagues were so determined to defend British sovereignty from Berlin and yet so eager to share it with Paris. In the early stages of the Second World War, however, with our national life on the line, there can have been no doubts about the sense of the proposal. Nor can the context have left any doubt that the "Union" would be of limited duration. Churchill was offering "common citizenship *in this struggle*" (my italics). Once the struggle had been won, the Union would be put to bed. The motivation, the nature and the future of this Union were in British hands and our greatest patriot was therefore happy to be the driving force behind it. The problem, in the years since the Second World War, has been that Britain has never been in charge. Europe's politics have been formed in our absence and they have never been a good fit for us.

We have, broadly speaking, adopted four different attitudes towards the politics of European integration.

Firstly, there have been those who have noted the lack of sympathy between our worldview and the prevailing European worldview, and who have concluded from this that Britain should stand aside from Europe. Winston Churchill and Clement Attlee fall into this category. Secondly, there have been those who have decided that we should be involved but that Europe should be changed to meet our

---

[36]https://www.winstonchurchill.org/learn/speeches/speeches-of-winston-churchill/122-their-finest-hour

requirements. Pre-eminent in this group are Harold Macmillan and Margaret Thatcher. Shamefully, a third group has taken the view that we should deceive ourselves as to the realities of European politics and pretend that its manifold problems do not exist. Edward Heath takes the lead here. Finally, there have been those who believe that Britain should recast itself in the European mould and enter wholeheartedly into a United States of Europe.

In this chapter we will explore the first three of these different attitudes to Europe and begin to think about what we can learn from the various approaches. Firstly, however, we must understand one particularly important vision for Europe that emerged after the Second World War.

The wars of 1914–1918 and of 1939–1945 had visited the grimmest of horrors on Europe and Europeans. Across the continent there was a powerful determination that the nations of Europe should never again wage war against each other. Many in Europe agreed on how this was to be achieved; it seemed to them that the division of Europe into nation states was the problem and that, if only the nations of Europe could be merged into one bloc, the history of European war could be brought to an end. European unity was the answer.

Robert Schuman was the perfect person to champion such unity. He was France's foreign minister but he had a German surname and was of Luxembourg antecedents. In his own way he embodied European unity. In 1950, he published the Schuman Declaration[37] proposing a European federation and setting out a blueprint for how it should be achieved.

The necessary precursor to European unity, in Schuman's view, was "the elimination of the age-old opposition of France and Germany".

---

[37]http://europa.eu/about-eu/basic-information/symbols/europe-day/schuman-declaration/

With this in mind, Schuman's proposed first step was that "Franco-German production of coal and steel as a whole be placed under a common High Authority, within the framework of an organization open to the participation of the other countries of Europe". In Schuman's view, "[t]he solidarity in production thus established will make it plain that any war between France and Germany becomes not merely unthinkable, but materially impossible". Nor was this to be confined to France and Germany. Schuman wanted these coal and steel arrangements to be open to all countries willing to take part. These arrangements would, Schuman said, "lay a true foundation for...economic unification".

Schuman hoped that his proposal would "lead to the realization of the first concrete foundation of a European federation indispensable to the preservation of peace".

Schuman realised, however, that a united Europe could not be forged overnight: "Europe will not be made all at once, or according to a single plan. It will be built through concrete achievements which first create a de facto solidarity." Schuman went onto describe "[t]he pooling of coal and steel production" in Europe as "a first step in the federation of Europe".

One sometimes hears conspiracy theorists touting the idea that a shadowy cabal of Eurocrats decided to establish a federal European superstate and that, realising that the peoples of Europe would never allow them to do so, they deceitfully set out to unify Europe by a series of small, seemingly innocuous stages. That notion will not do. Schuman was absolutely upfront. His declaration clearly states that he wanted a European federation. It also lays out his plan to get there by a series of incremental stages. The European Coal and Steel Community was founded to be the first step. Many in Europe were happy to sign up to this idea. Britain was not.

There were two reasons for this: the first was the nature of the ECSC proposal and the second was Britain's conception of its role in Europe. We will look at both issues in turn.

The ECSC clearly had the grandest of ambitions: peace in Europe. Its aim was to use the most crucial forces of a country's economy to determine the most important questions of its foreign policy. The difficulty was that if you had sat down and tried to design a scheme that would be anathema to post-war Britain you could not do better than the Schuman Plan. After all, we had paid the highest of prices to safeguard our sovereignty; were we now to give it away?

There was also considerable fear that the practicalities of the ECSC would not work in our favour. Thinking of the possible effect on our coal industry, Lord Morrison dismissed the suggestion that Britain join the ECSC with the words: "the Durham miners won't wear it". The foreign policy issues were no less major. However regrettable it may have been, the lesson of the twentieth century thus far seemed to be that Britain needed the freedom to wage war in Europe if necessary. What would have been the result, after all, if we had been linked in a coal and steel community with Nazi Germany?

There was also the issue of the democratic deficit in the proposed organisation. As Prime Minister, Clement Attlee made Britain's position clear. Speaking in a House of Commons debate on 27 June 1950, Attlee said that his Government was "not prepared to accept the principle that the most vital economic forces of this country should be handed over to an authority that is utterly undemocratic and is responsible to nobody"[38]. Most seemed to agree with Attlee that the ECSC was so bedevilled by institutional flaws that it was not an organisation that Britain could join. Many more would have agreed with Winston Churchill that the ECSC was (as its name

---

[38] http://hansard.millbanksystems.com/commons/1950/jun/27/schuman-plan-1

suggests) designed for European states and that, frankly, Britain was rather more than simply a European state.

Churchill famously said that he wanted to see "a kind of United States of Europe"[39]. British Europhiles sometimes deploy this quote to bathe their pro-Europeanism in the warm glow of patriotism. They imply that because Churchill spoke in favour of European unity he wanted Britain to join in. He did not. In same speech wherein Churchill referred to a United States of Europe he stated clearly that he wanted Britain and the Commonwealth to stand with the United States and, ideally, with Soviet Russia as the "friends" and the "sponsors" of a European union. There is no evidence that he had any interest in Britain actually joining such an organisation. Churchill believed that Britain had a global role and destiny. Most of Churchill's countrymen agreed with him. By force of geography, European politics would always be of great importance to us but what we really wanted was for the Europeans to conduct themselves calmly and quietly so that we could be spared any regional noises-off while we were trying to assert ourselves amongst the superpowers. This idea allowed us to feel comfortable in spurning the ECSC. If we were busily occupied on the global stage then we could feel confident that we did not need any particular continental focus. If, however, our view of our global role were to prove misguided, we would probably need to reassess our European policy. Suez would prompt just such a reassessment.

The Suez Crisis exploded the myth that Britain was in the same league as the superpowers. Though a military success, Suez was a political, economic and moral disaster. In response to Colonel Nasser's invasion, Britain, France and Israel concocted a duplicitous plan whereby the Israelis would invade and, under the guise of separating the Israelis and the Egyptians, the British and the French would themselves invade and retake the Canal. The first part of the

[39]http://www.churchill-society-london.org.uk/astonish.html

plan worked perfectly and, not long after the initial troop landings, the path to the Canal was clear. Beyond the Canal Zone, however, the situation was in freefall. We had been abandoned by the Commonwealth and actively undermined by the United States. The Americans began to dump Sterling and the Pound's value plummeted. Ironically, given that one of the reasons for trying to take back the Canal was to secure our oil supply, the collapse in our currency left us unable to buy oil in the international markets. We needed dollars and the US would only provide them if we pulled out of Suez. Left with no choice, we capitulated. It was the end of Britain's unofficial Empire in the Middle East and exposed the limitations to our ability independently to defend our overseas interests. Suddenly, our global role looked precarious (not to say preposterous). This was to have major implications for our relationship with our nearer neighbours.

Gone was the idea that we had any value as Europe's "sponsor". Europe, however, might have value to us. The ECSC had by now become the European Economic Community. The economies of the EEC member states were growing more quickly than ours and the opportunities for trade were not to be sniffed at. There was also the possibility that we might together represent a formidable anti-Communist alliance. If we could not be an independent global power, a strong relationship with Western Europe began to look more important. However, if Britain had changed since the late 1940s, so had European politics. And not for the better.

The anti-democratic tendencies of the ECSC had not been diminished in the transformation into the European Economic Community; it had become worryingly inward-looking and agriculture-focussed. Britain's trade links were global rather than simply continental and our farming sector was smaller than the European average. The EEC had not been designed with us in mind and, much as we might now want greater involvement in Europe, we were far from convinced that the EEC would do the trick. Prime Minister Harold Macmillan was clear that, though he was in favour of Britain playing a more active role in mainstream European politics, Britain could not sign up to the EEC as it then stood. If we were to pursue a relationship with the EEC, the EEC would have to change. Britain would need special terms for trade with the Commonwealth (and beyond) as well as recognition that our farming sector was smaller than the European norm and that this should be reflected in our membership fee.

So, could we get our terms? Alas, the answer was no – or rather "non"– thanks to French President Charles De Gaulle. De Gaulle recognised that the EEC would be a poor fit for Britain but he had no intention of allowing the EEC to change in order to accommodate us. In De Gaulle's view it was "possible that one day England might manage to transform herself sufficiently to become part of the European community, without restriction, without reserve and preference for anything whatsoever"[40] but one thing was for sure: as far as De Gaulle was concerned it was Britain that would have to do the transforming, not Europe.

The result was an impasse. Britain would not join the EEC unless the EEC changed and the EEC would not have Britain unless Britain changed. It was less than ideal but at least it was honest. The problem came when dishonesty crept into the mix. That came with Edward Heath.

Edward Heath was no fool. He was a bright man and an able politician. He saw that British membership of the EEC would be uncomfortable and fraught with issues. Nevertheless, he also took the view that we would still be better off in than out. Whether or not one agrees with it, that was and remains a perfectly coherent view.

---

[40] Quoted in van Middelaar, Luuk, *The Passage to Europe: How a Continent Became a Union* Yale University Press, 2013 Page 170

A bad option can still be better than all the others and international politics does sometimes mean choosing the lesser of two evils. Heath could have put the case in those terms. He could have said: "The EEC is far from ideal and there will be plenty of drawbacks if we join – but things will be even worse if we do not join." The history of Britain's membership of the EEC of the European Community and of the European Union might have been very different had our original membership been discussed in these honest terms. Sadly, Heath chose deception over candour and, in doing so, poisoned British–European relations.

Heath told the House of Commons that "There will not be a blueprint for a federal Europe"[41]. He knew this to be untrue. Indeed, in his speech he went onto say that several members of the Community did want a federal system but that they had been persuaded "to forgo their federal desires so that Britain should be a member and take part in political consultation and co-ordination with them". The muddled thinking here is plain to see. Either there is no blueprint, or there is a blueprint but it has been shelved. It is a matter of linguistic logic that only one of those statements could be true; it was a matter of political fact that both were false. Heath told us that we were joining a free trade area and that federalism was not on the agenda. It was a lie.

The relationship between Britain and the EEC/EC/EU was always going to be difficult but this ugly falsehood meant that it got off to the worst possible start. Britain would soon feel betrayed as Europe moved towards a superstate that we had thought was off the cards; Europe gained a new member that always stood in the way of political progress. Britain is wrong, however, to blame the EU. The direction of travel was clear when we joined. The betrayal was Heath's, not Europe's. Nevertheless, now that we were in, we would

---

[41] http://hansard.millbanksystems.com/commons/1970/feb/25/britain-and-the-european-communities

have to make the best of it. Initial efforts to secure a better deal came to nothing (whatever he said, Harold Wilson's renegotiation plumbed the very depths of failure) but there was one British leader with the strength to assert British interests in Europe: Margaret Thatcher.

If General de Gaulle had said "Non" to Britain, Mrs Thatcher famously said "No, no, no!" to Europe. She had no great love for the Continent. Her understanding of twentieth-century history was that Europe had been rather better at supplying problems than at providing solutions, and that it had been the English-speaking peoples who had been left to pick up the pieces. Mrs Thatcher could express this opinion sharply. At a Downing Street reception she met a backbench Tory MP who was downcast after England had lost to Germany at football. "Isn't it awful Prime Minister," remarked the MP, "the Germans have beaten us at our own national game." "Never mind dear," came the reply, "we beat them twice at theirs." This attitude underpinned her approach to European politics. She was determined to beat them at their own game. The first round was budget negotiations.

As we have seen, one reason why EEC membership was such a poor fit for Britain was that our agricultural sector was considerably smaller than that of the other EEC members. This was a problem because agriculture absorbed a vast proportion of the EEC's spending. An EEC state with lots of farmers was thrilled by this; they would receive bumper sums from the EEC. Britain was considerably less chuffed. We had far fewer farmers and it was therefore much more difficult for the EEC to spend money within our shores. Despite the fact that we were not getting much back from the EEC we were still required, under the rules of the time, to make huge payments to the EEC's budget. The result was that Britain made a massive net contribution to the EEC. This was unfair in any case but was ludicrously so when you consider that, at the time, we were one of the EEC's poorer states. Heath had signed us up for this and the situation had survived Wilson's renegotiation. It would not survive Mrs Thatcher.

The first battle over the rebate took place at the EEC's Dublin summit at the end of 1979. The Prime Minister told her continental colleagues that the status quo was unacceptable and that she wanted "our money" back. Having told them this once, she told them again. And again. And again. The German Chancellor pretended to fall asleep. The French President ordered his motorcade pull up outside and start revving its engines. Mrs Thatcher's response? She told them again. Initially, as she must have expected, she got nowhere.

Minimal progress was made at Dublin and Mrs Thatcher got little further at the Luxembourg summit in 1980. She picked up the point again in Stuttgart and then in Athens. The other leaders tried to ignore her and they tried to fob her off; these were not tactics to try on the Iron Lady. The nature of the discussion put Mrs Thatcher in a strong position. Britain was paying lots more to the EEC than she was getting back in EEC payments. The Prime Minister therefore wanted us to be given an extra payment from the EEC so that our net contribution would not be so large. Getting an extra payment back was obviously one way of reducing the size of our net contribution but, if the Europeans would not discuss that, then there was another option: we could stop paying the money to the EEC in the first place. Mrs Thatcher began to hint that this might be a possibility. Regretfully she came to realise that she would not get this through the House of Commons, but the threat had helped push matters over the edge.

At Fontainebleau in June 1984, after an epic session in the negotiating chamber, the principle of a British rebate was agreed. That just left the percentage. What proportion of our contribution should we get back? Mrs Thatcher wanted 70%. The others originally thought that 50% would be a more appropriate figure.

Mrs Thatcher stood firm. They offered 60%. No deal. They offered 65%. Still no deal – but 65% was within a reasonable distance of something Mrs Thatcher could agree: two thirds. And, for Mrs Thatcher, two thirds meant two thirds. There was some spurious suggestion that 66% would do. Mrs Thatcher explained that 66% most certainly would not do. 66% was not two thirds. Chancellor Kohl gave in: Britain could have 66.6% of its contribution back. One is almost left thinking that the 0.6% was the sweetest part of the victory.

The struggle over the rebate plays squarely into the Thatcher legend. Tough and determined, handbagging her opponents and battling for Britain. One must be wary, however, of reading too much into it. On the issue of the rebate it is true that she was fighting for Britain and (to the extent that Britain paying less would mean others paying more) she was fighting against the rest of the EEC. That was not always the case. Sometimes she fought for Britain *and* for the EEC. The debates about the Single Market were an example of this. In this instance she did not want Europe to carve out a special place for Britain – she wanted the rest of the EEC to change course as well. This, Mrs Thatcher firmly and rightly believed, was not just in Britain's interests (important though that was), it was also in the EEC's interests. Sadly the EEC could not recognise this and it was, therefore, a battle that Thatcher could not win. The battle to which I refer came over the implementation of the Single European Act and the future trajectory of European politics.

The principal basis of the Single European Act was a very good thing. Its main purpose was to introduce the Common Market so as to increase the volume of trade between the member states of the EEC. This was music to Mrs Thatcher's ears. She was itching to make it easier for British companies to gain access to European markets. She was also aware that competition from European firms would drive up standards across the board.

The Common Market was needed because, while the removal of various tariffs had effectively established an EEC free trade area, trade had not flourished as much as expected. The reason for this was that tariffs were not the only barriers to intra-EEC trade. The multiplicity of rules and regulations governing goods and services were just as troublesome. The variety of regulatory regimes meant that a French company whose business was producing, say, light bulbs might manufacture light bulbs that complied with all the relevant French rules and could legally be sold in France but might not meet the relevant standards anywhere else. The absence of tariffs is of no help here; the company would have completely to rejig its manufacturing process. The Common Market was designed to eliminate this problem by standardising the trade rules across the EEC.

Like free trade, standardised trade rules within a Common Market was a good idea and Mrs Thatcher was all for it. No European leader pushed as hard for its establishment. Obviously the Common Market meant a loss of sovereignty, but only over matters such as the rules governing the manufacture of light bulbs. When one weighs that loss against the commercial gain it seemed like a good bargain. Success seemed assured. Standardised rules would liberate business and turbo-charge European trade. Brussels regulation would be lauded as our passport to prosperity. -Or so we hoped. In fact, as we know, things turned out rather differently.

The devil, as ever, was in the detail. Standardised rules are a good thing in principle but can be very bad in practice. If, for instance, they are too light-touch then business can misbehave with the result that consumers, employees and, ultimately, business all lose out. If, on the other hand, the standardised rules are too burdensome they act as a restriction on trade so that business and, ultimately, consumers and employees lose out. As with Goldilocks' porridge, regulation needs to be 'just right'. Unfortunately, the EEC took the wrong course.

Regulation piled upon regulation. From the curvature of fruit to the length of the working day, there seemed to be nothing that was beyond the reach of the Common Market's lawmakers. Healthy economic activity was not encouraged but restrained. Mrs Thatcher was dismayed.

The Prime Minister had pushed and pushed and pushed her fellow heads of Government into agreeing to establish the Common Market. Then, in the aftermath of what should have been a triumph, she saw Brussels set about wrecking it. And that was not the only problem with the Single European Act.

In order to get the Common Market agreed as part of the Single European Act, Mrs Thatcher had to acquiesce as some very suspect clauses were included alongside the trade provisions. The Single European Act stated that there was a "responsibility incumbent upon Europe to aim at speaking ever increasingly with one voice". It also included a commitment to "making concrete progress towards European unity". There was also much mention of economic and monetary union and of endeavouring "jointly to formulate and implement a European foreign policy". The other heads of Government were taking these aspects of the Single European Act much too seriously.

Her European colleagues were dragging Mrs Thatcher into the worst of all possible worlds. They were making a hash of implementing the Common Market but being far too enthusiastic in pressing for European unity. With excessive regulation choking our economy and with calls for a European superstate growing ever more strident, Mrs Thatcher knew that it was time to fight back. Unlike the rebate, however, this was not about a special deal just for Britain. It was about persuading the other European leaders to adopt the British approach to European politics. Thatcher was trying to save Europe from itself. The most celebrated episode in this campaign came on 20th September 1988 at the College of Europe in Bruges.

In giving the Bruges Speech Mrs Thatcher was fully aware of how little Europe wanted to hear what she had to say. Early in her speech she addressed the College of Europe's chairman and remarked that he had invited her to speak on the subject of Britain and Europe. The Prime Minister then congratulated the chairman on his courage, saying that "If you believe some of the things said and written about my views on Europe, it must seem rather like inviting Genghis Khan to speak on the virtues of peaceful coexistence!"[42] Unpopular it may have been, but that would not stop Thatcher saying it. And she pulled no punches:

> "The Community is not an end in itself. Nor is it an institutional device to be constantly modified according to the dictates of some abstract intellectual concept. Nor must it be ossified by endless regulation.
>
> The European Community is a practical means by which Europe can ensure the future prosperity and security of its people in a world in which there are many other powerful nations and groups of nations".

The Prime Minister addressed the political point first:

> "My first guiding principle is this: willing and active cooperation between independent sovereign states is the best way to build a successful European Community.
>
> To try to suppress nationhood and concentrate power at the centre of a European conglomerate would be highly

[42] http://www.margaretthatcher.org/document/107332

> damaging and would jeopardise the objectives we seek to achieve.
>
> Europe will be stronger precisely because it has France as France, Spain as Spain, Britain as Britain, each with its own customs, traditions and identity. It would be folly to try to fit them into some sort of identikit European personality."

Later she turned to economics:

> "The aim of a Europe open to enterprise is the moving force behind the creation of the Single European Market in 1992. By getting rid of barriers, by making it possible for companies to operate on a European scale, we can best compete with the United States, Japan and other new economic powers emerging in Asia and elsewhere.
>
> And that means action to free markets, action to widen choice, action to reduce government intervention.
>
> Our aim should not be more and more detailed regulation from the centre: it should be to deregulate and to remove the constraints on trade."

In the concluding section of her speech (a section marked, tellingly, "The British Approach") she implored:

> "Let Europe be a family of nations, understanding each other better, appreciating each other more, doing more together but relishing our national identity no less than our common European endeavour."

Elsewhere in the speech she tackled the dispiriting trend towards protectionism, saying that the aim should be to reduce barriers to international trade rather than to build new ones. She also made it clear that Europe's role in defence must be rooted in NATO.

Thatcher's was a fine vision. It was sensible, it was practical – and it was doomed to failure.

Schuman's legacy lived on and the drive towards European unity had gained too much momentum. European leaders noted Mrs Thatcher's views, and pressed on regardless. It would be many years before Britain made another attempt to shape Europe's future.

Mrs Thatcher's immediate successors as Prime Minister took the view that the EU could not be changed and that the best that we could hope for would be to carve out a special place for ourselves within it. Hence John Major's opt-outs and Tony Blair's red lines. Things only began to improve when David Cameron came to power.

Some will never forgive Cameron for ditching his "cast-iron guarantee" to hold a referendum on the Lisbon Treaty but he has been a powerful figure in recent European history. Not only has he vetoed an EU Treaty but, even more remarkably, he managed to secure a cut to the EU's budget. He has also set out a radical programme for European reform.

Too many people think that the Prime Minister promised to renegotiate the terms of Britain's membership of the EU. That, however, is simply a fallback position in the event that his greater aim of EU-wide reform is not achieved. In his January 2013 Bloomberg speech, Cameron set out his first and preferred option. It consisted of five sensible principles for the next stage of the EU's political development: (i) competitiveness, (ii) flexibility, (iii) power being able to flow back to Member States as well as away from them, (iv) democratic accountability and (v) fairness. He then very clearly said:

> "My strong preference is to enact these changes for the entire EU, not just for Britain.

> But if there is no appetite for a new Treaty for us all then of course Britain should be ready to address the changes we need in a negotiation with our European partners."

Cameron wants to change the very basis on which the EU operates. Only if he cannot do that is he interested in changing the basis on which Britain operates in the EU. This is absolutely the right ambition but, as with so many fine ambitions, the difficulty will be in the execution. In the concluding chapter we will examine the reforms for which we should be campaigning and how we should go about it. And we will ask whether the Europeans will listen.

A British Manifesto for Europe

"We can do most good for Europe by being resolutely British. By showing Europe the way to go rather than trotting at Europe's heels". So said fictional Prime Minister Francis Urquhart in the BBC's dramatisation of Michael Dobbs' novel, *The Final Cut*. FU was quite right. As we have seen in the preceding chapters, Britain has had a long and complicated relationship with Europe and a proper study of this history furnishes us with a wealth of experience to use in devising a strategy. There are a number of points that we must bear in mind. The first of these points relates to sovereignty.

As we have seen from John and the Golden Bull and from Charles I and the Treaty of Dover, a country's political sovereignty is not always safe in the hands of that country's leaders. Had we been more aware of our history we might have been more sceptical of Wilson, Heath and their rosy promises. Nor, had we paid heed to Stephen Gardiner's experience of the Spanish Match, would we have put so much faith in opt-outs and red lines; in battles between legal form and political reality, the latter is always in the stronger position.

National instinct, however, runs deeper than historical knowledge and, as John found with the Revolutionary Barons and as Charles found with the House of Commons (and as Mary would have found one way or another had she lived longer), when we discover that we have been duped, we fight back with a vengeance. Those campaigning vigorously for us to leave the EU are part of a proud and noble tradition. They also have a very strong argument.

We have lost a good deal of sovereignty to Europe. Vast swathes of our law are written in Brussels and huge sums of our money are spent at Brussels' whim. It is clear that the EU wants to deepen ties even further and to see Britain subsumed into a United States of Europe. We must keep a close eye on questions of sovereignty and, whatever happens, we are going to need some sovereignty back.

The importance of keeping a tight grip on sovereignty, however, is not the only lesson that we should learn from our history. Important though it undoubtedly is, sovereignty must be considered alongside the question of how best to serve our national interest. As we have seen, both the Glorious Revolution and the Hanoverian Succession entailed drastic compromises of sovereignty. The best judgment, however, is that these compromises were worthwhile because, overall, these events served our national interests. There was a balance to be struck and I agree with the majority view that, in both instances, we got a good deal. That raises the question of whether the compromises of sovereignty that are involved in EU membership are justified by the wider improvements to our national interest. Is that the case?

On present terms it is almost impossible to be certain. The facts and figures are unavoidably unclear (after all, we can never know for sure how much better or worse off we would now be if we were not in the EU) and much is susceptible to personal interpretation. Rather like the Mona Lisa's expression, two people can look at the same thing and come to quite different opinions. Take trade. If we left the EU altogether our exporters would have to pay at least some tariffs on exports to the EU. That would represent a cost of leaving. But would that mean that these companies would be pushed into developing other foreign markets more actively and, if so, might there actually be a net gain to our departure? Leaving would free us up to reduce regulation at home but the EU would still be our greatest trading partner and, to the extent that our businesses wanted to trade with Europe, they would be bound by many of the relevant rules anyway (and, in our absence, one dreads to think what these would be).

If we left we would certainly save the extremely hefty membership fee. On its own terms that is a very considerable plus. On the other hand, our ready access to the Common Market is a major reason why we attract so much foreign direct investment. If we left the EU we would lose this advantage and become less attractive to foreign companies. Thousands of jobs could be at risk. We might, of course, be able to save money but it would put many livelihoods in jeopardy.

There is also a broader point about our role and status in a changing world. In this regard it is helpful to consider the EU alongside NATO. Nobody doubts that Great Britain is a major military power; but nobody doubts that we also benefit greatly from being a leading member of the world's mightiest military alliance. Similarly we may be confident in our status as a great economic power, but we may also be sure that it is useful to be a leading member of the world's largest trading bloc. The EU is India's second largest trading partner and the EU is the largest trading partner of the United States and China. There is an extent to which our membership of the EU strengthens our hand in dealing with all these three important states. That said, it is fair to ask whether the EU strengthens our hand as much as it should.

We want to do more business with India, the US and China but none of them are as open to trade as we would wish them to be. In theory we should find it easier to open doors in these countries if we can use some of the EU's economic muscle. Sadly, however, the EU does not seem particularly keen to exert itself in his regard. Arguably, therefore, we might do better trying by ourselves.

Nobody argues that the EU is ideal as it is and everybody agrees that we could get on perfectly well outside the EU. At present the arguments for "Remain" and "Leave" are finely balanced. However, when one looks at the sacrifices that we have made in respect of sovereignty and considers these alongside the EU's manifest failure to devote itself to economic growth, it is reasonable to find oneself leaning towards "Leave". Before we vote to quit the EU, however, we should ask whether there is anything more that we can do to make the EU deliver for Britain. Remember, after all, what we can learn from Palmerston and Salisbury: we do not have to accept the status quo. Under Palmerston and Salisbury, Britain was an active and positive player in Europe. Europe as a whole benefitted because Britain had the right ideas together with the will to champion them. We need that approach again today. We should, until 23rd June, be thinking not of "Remain" or "Leave" but of "Remain" or "Leave" or "Improve". And we should focus on the "Improve". There is a host of ways in which the EU could be reformed both so that it is more congenial to Great Britain and so that it can better serve the peoples of Europe.

In this chapter we will review some of the reforms that we should be seeking, we will examine why the weeks and months leading up to the United Kingdom's EU referendum is the perfect time to argue for these reforms and we will explore the most effective ways in which we can make our case.

First then to the reforms that we need to see. The EU has a vast array of problems and we cannot hope to solve them all. In particular we must leave it to members of the Eurozone and Schengen area to deal with their particular difficulties. That still leaves us, however, with much to do. We should focus on the economy and on sovereignty

The first economic challenge is to tackle excessive regulation. It is not just holding back British business, it is restraining commerce across the Continent. It piles costs onto business and stops them creating jobs. To be fair, nobody is actively in favour of excessive regulation. The problem is that nobody ever quite gets round to dealing with it. The answer is to impose a deadline. The UK should set up a consultation process giving businesses across the EU three months in which to set out what regulatory changes they would like to see. The Foreign and Commonwealth Office could review these responses and make suggestions for a suitably brutal cull of unnecessarily burdensome rules. We could then offer these reforms to the EU and see if any Member States wished to oppose them. If so we could give them three months to explain why they are opposed to the promotion of economic growth.

The second point is to engage much more openly with the rest of the world. For all its problems, the EU is still a major trading power. On some analyses it is a greater economic force than the US or China and on any reasonable analysis it can, where trade is concerned, speak to those countries on at least equal terms. European companies need access to markets in the US, in China and in India and, acting together through the EU, the countries of Europe can strike a good deal for our businesses and get them the new customers that they need. Estimates vary but some say that a free trade deal with the US could add €120 billion to the EU's economy. This is worth pursuing. Again, we should set deadlines and we should expect regular progress reports. We should make named officials responsible for pushing forward this agenda, and we should hold them accountable if they fail.

Alongside this we need to extend the Common Market. Services and energy are expanding markets and intra-European free trade in these areas can only be good for overall growth.

These three economic steps should be taken immediately and concurrently and will help address the European economic crisis. They will not, however, address the political crisis. Tackling that requires proper democratic reform. We should remember the Magna Carta Barons, the efforts of Bishop Gardiner and the work of Charles II's last Parliament – and we should push for the restoration of powers to the EU's member states.

European democracy has proved to be a non-starter and the absence of any meaningful demos means that such a democracy is unlikely to get off the ground anytime soon. National Parliaments must, therefore, step into the fray. Ideally we would do away with the European Parliament altogether but that is probably a bridge too far at this stage. There are two steps, however, that should be taken now.

Firstly we need a system whereby national Parliaments could, collectively, take the place of the European Parliament on certain issues. There would be a mechanism whereby members of national Parliaments could inform the European Parliament that they wanted to take control on a particular piece of legislation and, if a sufficient number of national Parliamentarians took this course then the debates and votes that would have taken place in the European Parliament would take place in national Parliaments. The process would take longer as there would need to be two debates in each national Parliament (the second would be needed so that each Parliament could consider the points made in the others) but it would mean that genuinely accountable Parliamentarians would hold open debates on the major issues. Power would begin to flow back to the Member States and to their peoples.

Secondly national Parliamentarians should also take a much more important role in reviewing EU spending and in challenging EU waste. Too much EU spending is a testament to what happens when you mix profligacy with incompetence and do not bother to supervise them. The EU's money comes from the citizens of its member states and the Parliamentarians of those member states should monitor that spending and highlight any waste. Hopefully the discipline imposed by knowing that their spending will be the subject of proper scrutiny will improve the quality and efficiency of EU spending. Not only should this save us money but, as national Parliamentarians and the peoples of Europe begin to look more carefully at what the EU is doing, they might just begin to wonder whether it is doing the right things. Such a consideration of the EU's present activities can only bode well for an analysis of what the EU should do in the future. Combined with the measures set out above, this will go a long way towards improving the operation of the EU. The British Government has insisted that public officials publish details of all spending over £500. We should have the same level of transparency over there as we have here. Remember Pitt the Younger saying that England "saved herself by her exertions and will, as I trust, save Europe by her example"? Well, as the Eurocrats would say: *plus ça change...*

Even if we take them together these steps will not create a perfect EU. There would still be a host of other issues needing to be addressed. The Common Agricultural Policy is in a mess and the Common Fisheries Policy is little better. Most important of course, is the euro. No one can predict how the euro crisis will develop, or even how long the EU will be around. Undoubtedly the single currency is in for a rough time and, if it is to survive at all, will need radical reform. Inevitably the euro will absorb a great deal of attention; what we must not allow is for the EU to monopolise European political discussions. Whatever happens to the single currency, Europe's future looks bleak indeed unless we carry out the three economic and two political reforms outlined above.

These, then, are the reforms for which Britain should be pressing. The next question is whether we will persuade the Europeans to listen. It is only fair to acknowledge that the precedents in this regard are far from good.

Macmillan tried to persuade Europe to mend its ways. He failed. So did Wilson. Thatcher had success over the rebate but her Bruges Speech remained an unfulfilled wish list. Major, Blair and Brown were content to accept the EU as it was and try to operate on special terms. Cameron, it is true, has had his victory over the budget but that does not guarantee that he will have any have success regarding the much more fundamental matters that now fall to be decided. Britain has wanted a different kind of Europe for years and has always been disappointed; why should things be any different this time? The answer is that time has moved on and that Britain has been shown to be right.

Whereas hitherto we have been dealing in predictions, now we are dealing in facts. Just by way of a brief excursus, consider the British attitude at the Messina Conference of 1955. The Messina Conference had been convened to start the process of turning the European Coal and Steel Community into the European Economic Community. Britain was invited to attend on the basis that, while we had not joined the ECSC, we might be interested in joining the EEC. We were not. According to legend, the British representative, Russell Bretherton, told his fellow delegates: "Gentlemen, you're trying to negotiate something you will never be able to negotiate. If negotiated, it will not be ratified. And if ratified, it will not work". The Europeans, clearly, disagreed. They thought that the EEC would be a riotous success. Neither Bretherton nor the other Messina delegates could offer proof positive that their forecast would come true and the EEC proceeded on the basis that the British would be wrong. Perhaps history could have turned out differently but the fact is that it has not. Europe's current economic and political settlement is a failure.

Look at the economy. The EU as a whole was in recession for most of 2011-2013. Growth since then has been patchy and a number of EU economies have seen negative economic growth even in the midst of this feeble recovery. According to the EU's own figures, over 22 million EU citizens were unemployed in October 2015 and just over 4.5 million of them were under 25. Who looks at this and says "steady as she goes"?

Nor are things better if one takes a broader political view.

In 2005 the French and the Dutch rejected the EU Constitution in referenda. In 2011 there was anger in Ireland as details of the Irish budget were disclosed to the German Bundestag before the Irish Parliament. More recently rioters in Greece have burnt the EU's flag while Cypriot protestors have likened Chancellor Merkel to Hitler. More recently the migration crisis has put tremendous pressure on the Schengen Area. Across the EU, far right parties are on the rise.

The idea that the peoples of Europe are so in love with the EU that they are blind to its flaws is self-evidently nonsense. Across Europe people are concerned about the economy and they are anxious that their national sovereignty is being eroded. History has proved Britain right. We are no longer saying, as Bretherton said, "It will not work". We are now able to say that it has not worked and is not working. This makes our position stronger than it has ever been before and that is why, finally, we have a good chance to recast the EU into a more sensible form.

So how are we to go about championing these reforms? The lesson here is from Pitt the Younger and Wellington. We will need a coalition.

Just as Napoleon was only beaten by a coalition of European powers under British leadership, so now Britain should form, and lead, a coalition to reform the EU. Unlike the coalitions known to Pitt and Wellington, however, this coalition will not, initially, be a coalition of states and politicians. If it is to work, it will have to be a coalition of peoples.

This is where David Cameron needs to change his approach. During the renegotiation phase of proceedings he focussed on trying to persuade Europe's political class of the need for reform. He did much better than expected but it was never likely that he would make huge progress with his fellow heads of government. Europe's political elite has long demonstrated a spectacularly stubborn refusal to acknowledge the failures that have so angered the peoples of Europe. There is also the problem that the debate has become adversarial. It is being presented as a contest between Britain and Europe. This is not only unhelpful; it is inaccurate. The reforms that Great Britain wishes to see would not only help Britain; they would benefit citizens in all member states. If Britain "wins" the argument over these reforms then the rest of the EU would win too.

What is needed is a change of tack. It is time to bypass the elites. The peoples of Europe already understand the problems facing the EU and it is therefore to the peoples of Europe that appeals for reform should be made. Cameron should reach out to those business groups and journalists in each member state who will be able to found and operate pro-reform campaigns in their own countries. The arguments should be put in resolutely positive terms. The Prime Minister must emphasise that these proposals would benefit the EU as a whole. Some will have doubts about supporting British-led reforms but, with time, they could be won over (a Twitter hashtag along the lines of "#theBritshaveapoint" might be helpful). After all, the arguments for reform are not complicated. If you want jobs, economic growth and democratic accountability then the reforms described above are not "nice to haves"; they are absolute essentials. As support for these reforms grows, so vote-hungry politicians will begin to get on side and the necessary steps will be taken.

Timing will be of vital importance. If recent British experience is anything to go by, there will be two stages to the EU negotiations. The first stage was the round of talks before the date of the vote was announced. The second is the period of campaigning in the run-up to polling day on 23rd June. We saw this in the 2014 Scottish referendum. As the campaign progressed, the argument moved on dramatically. Only two days before the referendum, the leaders of the three main Westminster parties made their "Vow" of more powers for the Scottish Parliament if Scotland remained in the United Kingdom. The EU referendum could conceivably follow a similar programme. If so, Cameron should be prepared to make the most of the second stage of the process. It is at this stage that public opinion in the EU more broadly could be of most use. Here again, there is a lesson to be drawn from the Scottish referendum

In 2014, the people of England became more interested in the issues as the campaign went on. Debate about the future of the United Kingdom came to be almost as common south of the border as it was in Scotland. We could well see something similar in the EU referendum. It is likely that an "In/Out" referendum in a major EU member state will capture headlines and attention across the continent. As the debate comes to the fore, there will be a greater chance of winning widespread support for EU reform. That support should help convince EU leaders to offer the sort of change that the EU needs to see.

This would be one of the most extensive exercises of democratic power in European history. It will be no small undertaking and it needs to happen quickly. It will not happen at all without Britain.

Britain can see that the EU needs to enact radical reform if it is to start delivering for the peoples of Europe. The EU should give powers back to national parliaments, it should cut regulation and it should pursue free trade deals across the world. Such reforms would turn the EU into the prosperity-focussed organisation that Britain has always wanted it to be. It would be in the interests of all EU member states for the EU to effect this transformation. If, even with Britain heading towards the exit, the EU cannot mend its ways it will be sending us a clear sign that the EU is not the right place for Britain. If so, we should be confident in our ability to thrive outside the EU.

If the EU refuses to change then Britain may well leave. If the EU takes its lead from Britain then we might remain and the EU as a whole will be better off. As so often before, Britain is ready to lead. The question is whether Europe is ready to follow.

Bibliography

Breay, Claire, *Magna Carta Manuscripts and Myths*, The British Library, 2002

Bryant, Arthur, *The Story of England – Makers of the Realm*, Reprint Society by arrangement with William Collins, Sons & Co. Ltd.

Chamberlain, Muriel E, *Lord Palmerston*, GPC Books, 1987

Churchill, Winston S, *A History of the English-Speaking Peoples*, Weidenfeld & Nicolson 2002

Gibson, Robert, *Best of Enemies: Anglo-French Relations Since the Norman Conquest*, Impress Books Limited, 2004

Hague, William, *William Pitt the Younger*, HarperCollinsPublishers, 2004

Hibbert, Christopher, *Disraeli A Personal History*, HarperCollinsPublishers, 2004

Hurd, Douglas and Young, Edward, *Disraeli or The Two Lives*, Weidenfeld & Nicolson 2013

Mowat, RB, *A Short History of Great Britain Since 1714*, Oxford University Press 1928

Simms, Brendan and Riotte Torsten (eds) *The Hanoverian Dimension in British History, 1714–1837*, Cambridge University Press 2007

Roberts, Andrew, *Salisbury Victorian Titan*, Phoenix 2000

Thorpe, DR, *Supermac, The Life of Harold Macmillan*, Chatto & Windus 2010

Wilson, Harold, *A Prime Minister on Prime Ministers*, Weidenfeld & Nicolson 1977

van Middelaar, Luuk, *The Passage to Europe: How a Continent Became a Union* Yale University Press, 2013

Whitelock, Anna, *Mary Tudor England's First Queen*, Bloomsbury 2010

ND - #0247 - 080726 - C0 - 229/152/15 - PB - 9781784563318 - Gloss Lamination